Projecting 9/11

Perspectives on a Multiracial America Series
Joe R. Feagin, Texas A&M University, Series Editor

Projecting 9/11

Race, Gender, and Citizenship in Recent Hollywood Films

Mary K. Bloodsworth-Lugo and
Carmen R. Lugo-Lugo

ROWMAN & LITTLEFIELD
Lanham • Boulder • New York • London

Published by Rowman & Littlefield
A wholly owned subsidary of The Rowman & Littlefield Publishing Group, Inc.
4501 Forbes Boulevard, Suite 200, Lanham, Maryland 20706
www.rowman.com

Unit A, Whitacre Mews, 26–34 Stannery Street, London SE11 4AB, United Kingdom

British Library Cataloguing in Publication Information Available

Library of Congress Cataloging-in-Publication Data
Bloodsworth-Lugo, Mary K.
Projecting 9/11 : race, gender, and citizenship in recent Hollywood films / Mary K. Bloodsworth-Lugo and Carmen R. Lugo-Lugo.
pages cm — (Perspectives on a multiracial America series)
Includes bibliographical references and index.
ISBN 978-1-4422-1826-0 (cloth : alk. paper) — ISBN 978-1-4422-1828-4 (electronic)
1. September 11 Terrorist Attacks, 2001, in motion pictures. 2. Race in motion pictures. 3. Sex role in motion pictures. 4. Citizenship in motion pictures. 5. Motion pictures—United States—History—21st century. I. Lugo-Lugo, Carmen R. II. Title.
PN1995.9.T46B58 2014
791.43'6552—dc23
2014030141

∞ ™ The paper used in this publication meets the minimum requirements of American National Standard for Information Sciences Permanence of Paper for Printed Library Materials, ANSI/NISO Z39.48-1992.

Printed in the United States of America

Contents

Acknowledgments

This project is the outgrowth of a decade of work on the discourse surrounding the events of September 11, 2001, especially rhetorical techniques deployed by the G. W. Bush administration in response to the happenings of that day. Official presidential discourse was advanced and promoted in print media, television news, and films—including Hollywood productions—to frame the events of September 11, 2001, for an American public. This includes anxieties, fears, and insecurities of Americans in the wake of unprecedented events. The ideologies developed in the aftermath of September 11, 2001, form a *9/11 project*, whereby "9/11" evokes much more than happenings of a particular day. Rather, 9/11 issues an array of meanings and significances—not the least of which are those related to perceptions and conceptions of race, gender, and citizenship in a new and changed America.

We would like to thank Joe R. Feagin, series editor for *Perspectives on a Multiracial America*, for his sincere interest in this project and for including it within his impressive series. We also appreciate the helpful and constructive feedback of Professor Feagin, as well as anonymous peer reviewers, which helped to improve the manuscript. We are very grateful to Sarah Stanton, senior acquisitions editor at Rowman & Littlefield, for encouraging a monograph on these themes, and for her consistent generosity and assistance at all stages of development and completion. Mary would like to thank Selena K. L. Breikss for providing course assistance during fall 2013 which facilitated the book's completion. We are also grateful to our colleagues in the Department of Critical Culture, Gender, and Race Studies at Washington State University, especially Rich King, Lisa Guerrero, and David Leonard, for their ongoing and consistent support and friendship.

Chapter One

Introduction

We learn about the world and how the world is run through the mass media and popular culture. (Birkenstein, Froula, and Randell 2010, 11)

But what might be most culturally significant—and most affecting in so many ways—is exactly in what manner and to what degree "9/11" is becoming our cultural esperanto: our language of grief and anger, of loss and steadfastness. (Melnick 2009, 7)

In a Gallup poll conducted during the first quarter of 2010, Americans identified terrorism, along with federal government spending, as the most important threat faced by the United States. Of respondents, 79 percent indicated that terrorism was an extremely or a very serious threat to the country (Saad 2010). Later that same year, a *USA Today*/Gallup poll revealed that, for Americans, Republicans in Congress would do a better job than Democrats' handling seven of nine key election issues. The first issue listed was terrorism, with the strongest support for Republicans at 55 percent. The other six issues were immigration, federal spending, the economy, the situation in Afghanistan, jobs, and corruption in government (Jones 2010). It is worth noting that three of the seven issues (terrorism, the situation in Afghanistan, and immigration) are issues directly connected to the events of September 11, 2001.

This polling marked a departure from previous polling conducted since September 11, 2001, that consistently showed Americans considered Democrats to be more likely to handle most of these issues more effectively than Republicans (Jones 2010). The one solid exception concerned terrorism, which from May 2002 to August 2010 showed Americans consistently trusted Republicans over Democrats, with the exception of one poll conducted during October 2006 (Gallup 2013). In addition to the confidence in Republicans reflected by the 2010 *USA Today* /Gallup poll, the same poll showed that 75 percent of respondents identified terrorism as an extremely or very important issue when voting for congressional members that year.

The fact that nine years after the events of September 11, 2001, terrorism and related issues occupied such a prominent position in the collective mind of Americans, along with the consistent support for Republicans in Congress to handle this particular issue, reflects a totalizing rhetorical, ideological, and sociopolitical pattern (or project) emerging after the events of that day. We argue elsewhere that the G. W. Bush administration identified, constructed, and controlled threats to the country by attempting to "contain threatening bodies in 'new' and 'old' ways" (Bloodsworth-Lugo and Lugo-Lugo 2010, xiii). In this book, we name this particular effort the *9/11 project* , and in this introduction, we articulate the main features of the *9/11 project* and analyze its primary workings. We then aim to show how Hollywood feature films released after September 11, 2001, encapsulate and depict the *9/11 project* . As we explain below, mainstream feature films are direct products and reflections of the cultural moment in which they are created and thereby hold key insights about these very moments.

ARTICULATING THE *9/11 PROJECT*

When we refer to the *9/11 project*, we take into account the fact that since September 11, 2001, "9/11" has emerged as two related yet distinct notions: a historical marker recalling the horrific happenings of a particular day in U.S. history, and an institutionalized ideological, philosophical, and sociological construct encompassing more than a day and its particular events. As such a construct, we might say that "9/11" marks a multifaceted sociopolitical project involving the handling and containment of terrorism in particular and threats more generally. This project has involved the following enumerated efforts:

1. **The creation of key governmental institutions and policies aimed at managing and containing perceived threats to the United States and its people with a decidedly global reach.** These have included the Department of Homeland Security and the USA Patriot Act.
2. **Three war efforts.** One of these has been global and amorphous in scope (the War on Terror), while the other two (the wars in Afghanistan and Iraq) have been localized with global repercussions.
3. **Specific militarized sites in the United States and around the globe associated with the housing and management of terrorist and/or threatening bodies.** These have included the Guantanamo Bay detention camp, Abu Ghraib prison, and U.S. I.C.E. detention centers.
4. **Renewed nativist efforts at the federal and state levels seeking to restrict those deemed "un-American" from entering U.S. borders.** These have included the building of a fence separating the United States–Mexico international border, the deployment of military personnel to the United States–Mexico border, and Arizona's SB 1070.

5. **A paradigm shift in air travel**. This shift has included changes in screening and security, who is allowed at the gates, a revamping of the Transportation Security Administration (TSA) and its placement under the Department of Homeland Security, and changes in what can be carried onto airplanes by passengers.

6. **A consistent governmental rhetoric justifying items 1–5 on this list and creating an ideology around threats to the security of the country**.

The first five features constitute the political infrastructure of the *9/11 project*—an infrastructure designed with a global reach to ostensibly safeguard the local American population, while the sixth feature ascertains its sociocultural component. Together, they have become an omnipresent entity in U.S. society after September 11, 2001.

As part of its sixth feature, the *9/11 project* has included the development of ideologies, fears, anxieties, and perceptions—what Jeffrey Melnick (2009) has termed a "9/11 sensibility." It is 9/11 as a value-laden project of social and cultural import that drives the analytical pursuits of this book. Due to the durability and scope of these features, the ideological and sociopolitical project that is 9/11 has been revealed as having long-term impacts on Americans and their perceptions of threats, security, and even Americanness. From this perspective, 9/11 has been developed and engineered. As such, we argue that 9/11 was not present on, but rather emerged from, the events of September 11, 2001. Thus, to be clear and to differentiate the date of such events from the *9/11 project* as a broader construct, we use the full date (September 11, 2001) when we mean to reference the day or a historical moment, and we use 9/11 when we aim to discuss the sociopolitical and ideological project described above. We also use 9/11 as a descriptor (for example, 9/11 film and 9/11 society), and we use 9/11 instead of *post*-9/11 to emphasize that the *9/11 project* is still alive, relevant, and present tense.

An important component of the *9/11 project* is its effect on every aspect of U.S. culture and society, including cultural production. In his book *9/11 Culture*, Melnick proposes that as an event transformed into a concept, a discourse, and a language, 9/11 has served "as the answer to countless questions of social import," suggesting that 9/11 can be deployed to analyze and understand cultural and material production after September 11, 2001 (2009, 3). In *The Selling of 9/11*, Dana Heller tackles the material production of 9/11, arguing that September 11, 2001, was transformed "into a commercial pitch, a slogan" (2005, 2). Espousing a similar view to Melnick's idea of 9/11 as a material production, Heller states, "In the weeks and months following 9/11, the market for goods representing American patriotic unity and pride expanded dramatically" (6).

While these and other scholars consider ways in which September 11, 2001, has affected American culture, politics, society, and entertainment post-2001 (that is, ways in which 9/11 has emerged), we press this thesis to propose that the *9/11 project* has infected our collective imagination so thoroughly that it has become a primary lens through which Americans view the world around them. As with any other lens, the 9/11 lens is rooted in history, and as such, it can interact and even work in tandem with other lenses. In this case, we would specifically like to connect the *9/11 project* to Joe Feagin's *white racial frame*, which as he conveys, has been crafted over centuries of systemic racism and "extreme racial oppression" (2010, 2).

LINKING THE *9/11 PROJECT* TO THE *WHITE RACIAL FRAME*

According to Feagin, the *white racial frame* is a dominant frame with "an overarching white worldview that encompasses a broad and persisting set of racial stereotypes, prejudices, ideologies, images, interpretations and narratives, emotions, and reactions to language accents, as well as racialized inclinations to discriminate" (2010, 3). Feagin is clear that the *white racial frame* has global implications for our contemporary world racial order, a very important point, given the global reach of the *9/11 project*. Adia Harvey Wingfield furthers the analysis of systemic racism by offering the concept of "systemic gendered racism," explaining that manifestations of systemic racism are necessarily gendered, producing different outcomes for men and women of color (2009, 7). In particular, she argues that "inasmuch as racial oppression is continuing and fundamental in U.S. society, the 'racial dimensions' like racist ideology, racist imagery, and racist institutions that allow systemic racism to flourish are gendered" (7).

We agree with Wingfield that gender mediates systemic racism and would like to add that certain historical events are so powerful in their impact that they also mediate, if for a specific time, the racial and gendered dimensions allowing systemic racism to flourish. With such an impactful event, the *white racial frame* retains its main characteristics, but these also acquire specific inflections, especially when the event is transformed into a social project. We maintain that this is the case with 9/11 (event + project), through which systemic and gendered racism, and more specifically the *white racial frame*, have acquired particular emphases. Thus, we have modified the features identified by Feagin as belonging to the *white racial frame* in order to identify the 9/11 inflections to contemporary expressions of systemic gendered racism:

1. **Nonwhite bodies as terrorist threats**. After September 11, 2001, nonwhite groups in general and specific racialized groups such as Middle Easterners and Latinos have been depicted as suspicious and threatening to Americanness, which is rendered white. Members of these groups have been rendered destroyers of civilization and democracy.

2. **Consistent racial narratives about terrorism and terrorist bodies.** Terrorists have been said to "lurk in shadows" and "cross unprotected borders." Such narratives serve to justify the specific racialization of groups as threatening, presenting them as backward and animal-like (residing in caves, as rats in need of being "smoked out"), while simultaneously positioning U.S. society as a democracy seeking progress. Within this construct, progress is seen as an imperative of U.S. society. In turn, the United States is considered the ultimate purveyor of democracy ("the leader of the free world") in direct juxtaposition to backward countries that "harbor terrorists."

3. **Images and accents about racialized and threatening bodies as terrorist bodies.** These include photos released from Abu Ghraib, images from prisoners in Guantanamo, and language such as "enemy combatant" and "illegal immigrant." Images and accents help to create a specific discourse, reinforcing ideas about specific groups as threatening while reifying the whiteness of Americanness.

4. **Emotions and feelings toward brown bodies.** This point is best illustrated by the language of pundits and social commentators in relation to perceived terrorist, nonwhite, and/or immigrants bodies. This language creates emotional reactions to certain groups while reinforcing ideas developed by the previous features. In this process, singled-out groups are given a specific tone of threatening otherness by discourse and ideology. We discuss elsewhere how this process "has capitalized on United States fears and anxieties about public and national safety. Those located outside of United States' borders of security and comfort have been 'browned,' reinforcing fears and insecurities around them" (Bloodsworth-Lugo and Lugo-Lugo 2010, 73).

5. **Inclinations to discriminatory actions by individuals and institutions.** These include desecration of mosques, beatings

and harassment of suspected Middle Eastern men and women, the targeted suspension of civil liberties by the USA Patriot Act, and the "reasonable suspicion" clause in Arizona's SB 1070. These actions are justified, and sometimes even demanded, by the ideologies created via this process.

To Feagin's *white racial frame*, we would like to add a feature with a prominent role within the *9/11 project*. While implied within Feagin's framework, its prominence for our discussion in this book warrants a separate heading:

6. **The conflation of white and American**. Although not a new conflation, within 9/11 U.S. society, a terrorist threat to Americanness is a terrorist threat to whiteness. This conflation makes it easier to establish and justify an "us versus them" rhetorical strategy and even easier to distinguish between "browned" bodies and "Americans."

Finally, we argue that, as with the *white racial frame*, the *9/11 project* has a strong global component, in which, to reiterate, these features do not replace but rather work in tandem with the features of the original frame. Due to its lasting impact, we can locate the social and political project that is 9/11 (that is, the ideological and sociocultural concept developed as a response to the September 11, 2001, events) in most cultural artifacts produced after that date. These include U.S. mainstream films. In fact, as two-hour time capsules of our ideologies, Hollywood films produced after September 11, 2001, tend to feature the elements of the *9/11 project* described above—infrastructure and ideologies alike.

FILMS AFTER SEPTEMBER 11, 2001, AND THE *9/11 PROJECT*

In our view, many films released after September 11, 2001, have brilliantly embodied and advanced the *9/11 project*. A prominent aspect of this project is a rhetoric of "us versus them," involving multifaceted components promoted during the G. W. Bush presidency. Through articulations of terrorism and threat as "them" marking a threat to "us," President Bush discussed an axis of evil versus a coalition of the willing. He emphasized that a democratic society moves forward and embraces progress, whereas terrorist cells, training camps, and countries that "harbor terrorists" recall an undemocratic past. The Bush administration consistently reminded the American public that terrorism, terror, and terrorists ("them") are never far from Americans ("us").

In fact, if we review the four State of the Union addresses President Bush gave after his reelection in 2004, we find that he used the word "terrorist(s)" a total of fifty-seven times and "terror" a total of fifty-four times (for an average of thirteen to fourteen times per speech) (Presidential Rhetoric.com 2013). This rhetoric served to construct and reinforce the borders and boundaries between the categories "American" and "un-American"—categories that, since then, have invoked the nation but have likewise promoted gendered, racial(ized), and sexual(ized) notions. In a 9/11 United States, and through the *9/11 project*, protection, security, and the containment of threats have combined with matters of gender, race, and citizenship to become ideological tools for Americans' understanding of themselves and those around them. In 9/11 Hollywood films, we find both an examination of the events of September 11, 2001, and the operation of the ideological processes that have shaped the perceptions of Americans in a 9/11 world. As sources of meaning and influential carriers of reality, films have fostered the construction and comprehension of the *9/11 project* and 9/11 American culture.

Before we continue with our discussion of film, we should explain the naming for this group of films and how we have approached our selection and analysis. First, we refer to these films as 9/11 films, as opposed to *post*-9/11 films, not because these are films that depict the events of September 11, 2001, (although some do), but rather because these films reflect the *9/11 project* as explained above. Second, we have chosen to discuss films that in our estimation depict the *9/11 project* with the understanding that these are not the only films that depict that project, and in fact we maintain that a vast number of films might be construed as 9/11 films. Indeed, within some frameworks, all films released after September 11, 2001, might be considered such films. The films we have selected might also depict other projects, sensibilities, and frameworks, while at the same time, other films produced after September 11, 2001, might not depict the *9/11 project* as discussed in this book. These possibilities do not preclude the films analyzed here from being 9/11 films. It is not our intention to provide an exhaustive representation of what we call 9/11 films nor is it our intention to deny other lenses and frameworks. The films discussed in this book were chosen because each depicts a specific aspect of the *9/11 project*.

Mainly, we concentrate on the messages rehearsed by each of these films and the lessons delivered to viewers, regardless of whether or how these messages are received. Thus, we are not concerned with *how many* people viewed these films, or with *how much* critics liked or appreciated them, or with *the amount* of box office revenue they received. Rather, we are concerned with the tropes projected by the films, the ideas put forth, and the ideologies recreated. We also assume that the writers, producers, and directors creating these films are part and parcel of the society and time period in which they live. Some of the films we discuss here are about the events of September 11, 2001. Others depict the infrastructure of the *9/11 project*, including its wars. Others still are about futuristic scenarios and places invented by the Hollywood imagination, which at first glance, appear to have nothing to do with the events of September 11, 2001. However, as we demonstrate in our discussion, the messages in these films are inextricably tied to the *9/11 project*. In the end, we propose that our analysis in this book could be extended to other films, and to cultural productions more generally, released after September 11, 2001.

RACIALIZED GROUPS IN U.S. MAINSTREAM FILMS

In his seminal text *Film as Social Practice*, Graeme Turner asserts, "The reason we want to examine film at all is because it is a source of pleasure and significance [that is, meaning] for so many in our culture" (2006, 61). Jaap van Ginneken goes further by arguing that along with other genres of popular culture (such as television and music), films present a "forceful substitute [of] reality," for "sounds and images about other times and places convince us much more easily that this is how it probably is or was" (2007, 2–3). While we might wish to agree with van Ginneken's insight, we would argue that instead of being forceful *substitutes* for reality, films offer powerful ideological representations at a given time based on cultural perceptions of reality. Thus, it is not simply a matter of "this is how it probably is or was" but of "this is how 'we' perceive(d) it to be." As in any other context, perception thereby becomes reality. As sources of meaning and potentially influential perceptions of reality, films hold a key to comprehending the culture and time in which they are created. Andrew Schopp and Matthew B. Hill provide insight in relation to film (or popular culture more broadly) and perceptions after September 11, 2001, when they point out that "the events of September 11 and the subsequent War on Terror have further tangled the knotted relationship between popular culture, political discourse, and terrorism" (2009, 12).

In this book, we engage with ideologies and understandings developed as part of the *9/11 project* and ways in which those ideologies and understandings are projected in contemporary mainstream films, especially as they engage with issues of race, sexuality, gender, and citizenship. This is especially important in a country that has become a multiracial society, regardless of imperatives of whiteness. We examine specific ways in which recent Hollywood films have become both powerful sources of significance and forceful representations of reality in their portrayals and explanations of the events that unfolded on, and life and ideas after, September 11, 2001. These portrayals are often U.S. based; at other times, they are transnational; and at still other times, they encompass the globe. In main, our analysis aims to identify primary ideological components involving perceptions of reality after the events of September 11, 2001, as represented by one of the more influential means of cultural representation—mainstream films.

For over a century before the events of September 11, 2001, U.S. mainstream films had been developing and deploying ways of representing various minoritized social groups. Aided by standard techniques that included camera angles, lighting, and costumes, as well as dialogue and character development, the film industry disseminated very specific and consistent messages about racialized, gendered, and sexualized groups within U.S. society, including messages about what it means to be American (Vera and Gordon 2003). Hernán Vera and Andrew Gordon remark, "The image that [Americans] have of themselves is acquired by contrast to the images of others" (2003, 2). The messages concerning these groups is not entirely the invention of the film industry, clearly, for although groups have often been portrayed in ways unreflective of reality, the messages nonetheless have reflected, for the most part, the ideological underpinnings of the society at large. Vera and Gordon convey, "Hollywood spreads the fictions of whiteness around the world" (1). Further, as historical events have influenced ideologies and ideas about "different" groups within the larger society, these events have influenced the way groups have been presented in mainstream film. As Clara Rodríguez states, "The history of film is a microcosmic history of twentieth-century America, reflecting some of our best and worst moments as a nation" (2004, xi).

We can use the representation of racial(ized) groups in U.S. mainstream films to illustrate Rodríguez's point, since this topic has been well-researched and documented. Scholars have repeatedly shown the one-dimensional and stereotypical ways in which various ethnic groups have come to life in popular culture in general and in feature films particularly. From discreet constructions of Latino men as banditos, criminals, and evildoers, to constructions of Latinas as hot and sexy women of loose morals (Beltran 2009; Berg 2002), to constructions of Asian men as martial arts experts and Asian women as submissive, quiet servants—or conversely, as dangerous dragon ladies (Fuller and Gunning 2010), to representations of black men as criminals, Uncle Toms, and Sambos, to representations of black women as Mammies or Jezebels (Anderson 1997; Bogle 2001), to constructions of white men as saviors and white women as virtuous damsels (Bernardi 2001), the film industry had been diligent in crafting a variety of racialized representations. Without exception, representations of gender, sexuality, and citizenship in film have been mediated through the lens of race.

We contend that although we do witness aspects of these discreet gendered, sexualized, and racialized representations in Hollywood feature films after September 11, 2001—and perhaps more so in particular genres than others, such as animated children's films (see King, Lugo-Lugo, and Bloodsworth-Lugo 2010)—these more precise, if stereotypical, images have retreated as more generalized representations of "the other" have emerged. Of explicit concern in the 9/11 world has been "the terrorist other" as threat to Americanness. As we argue elsewhere, in the wake of the September 11, 2001, events, "particular bodies were constructed as American, while others were constructed as un- or anti-American," rendering the two as mutually exclusive and oppositional by definition (Bloodsworth-Lugo and Lugo-Lugo 2010, xxi).

A cursory look at U.S. history reveals that these oppositional constructions are not new, as there have been various moments in which Americanness has been articulated against and juxtaposed to un-Americanness based on the fears and ideologies of the time. For instance, during the first part of the twentieth century, Americanness was articulated in opposition to Communism/Communist ideals. A person who was deemed un-American was labeled Communist, not because he or she followed or believed in ideas associated with Communism, but because un-American and Communist effectively meant the same thing. This is why, when viewing graphic data depicting protestors seeking to preserve segregation as a way of life during the 1950s and '60s, we see many pictures of signs claiming "race mixing is Communism."

In general terms, as part of the *9/11 project*, Americanness is constructed in opposition to terrorism and terrorist threats. Conceptions about terrorism and terrorist threats are generated through notions of race, gender, sexuality, and citizenship, as well as the meanings associated with particular groups. As we argue elsewhere, since September 11, 2001, "the blending of otherwise distinct groups helped to underscore the proximity of terrorist threats to the average American" (Bloodsworth-Lugo and Lugo-Lugo 2010, 23). In 9/11 films, attention to race, gender, or citizenship shifts between and among categories, but these films adhere to a consistent framework of "us versus them"—the blueprint for the ideology of the *9/11 project*. The 9/11 other is clearly a threatening other and, more importantly, a global other. In fact, it is perhaps its global feature that lends the 9/11 other its slipperiness, making it difficult to identify the exact form of its threat. We are told that the 9/11 world is constantly in flux and movement (Bloodsworth-Lugo and Lugo-Lugo 2010). While noting this conception of flux, we are nonetheless able to outline the main contours of 9/11 Hollywood filmic representations of the newly articulated, but also derivative, American and un-American other.

These last two points concerning the global other and derivative articulations of Americanness and un-Americanness are of utmost importance, for they lend newer representations their 9/11 inflection. If someone were to ask, for instance, how 9/11 representations of Arabs in mainstream films are different from Orientalist-based representations of the 1980s and 1990s, our response would be that they are similar in content but different in scope. That is, there is a continuity of representation insofar as Arabs still play the role of terrorists, but there is a different reach for these characters. In a film such as *True Lies* (James Cameron), released in 1994, we see a direct portrayal of Arabs as terrorists; however, terrorism is a highly localized threat. In the film, terrorists (who operate in a local vacuum) threaten an area of the United States (Florida) and, even more specifically, the marriage of Harry and Helen Tasker (Arnold Schwarzenegger and Jamie Lee Curtis). We maintain that after September 11, 2001, cinematic constructions of terrorists are situated on a global scale. Terrorists never operate in a vacuum, and in fact the scope of their portrayal is global, even when the film's plot takes place in one or two settings. We can find telling examples of this in *Zero Dark Thirty* (Kathryn Bigelow, 2013) and *Lions for Lambs* (Robert Redford, 2007).

Similarly, although portrayals of American or Americanness also display continuities from previous times, 9/11 portrayals of Americanness display the following features: always under attack or being tested; always seeking, identifying, and battling another "lurking in shadows"; ultimately resolute. By contrast, the un-American (threatening) other is depicted as being everywhere (local and global); not subject to containment; adopting multiple and changing shapes; testing the core values of American democracy and progress (freedom, individuality, and demands for fairness or justice). Within this framework, the American assumes a stasis and reliability, while the un-American portrays a mutation and volatility.

Given the lasting repercussions of "the day that changed America," combined with the impact of that day's events on every aspect of American life (that is, the *9/11 project*), it remains important to examine and document ways in which ideologies developed and advanced after the September 11, 2001, events are reflected in and promoted by various cultural texts. Due to their pervasive nature, Hollywood mainstream films can be viewed as one of the better producers and products of culture, reflecting the understandings of the time period in which they are created. In this book, we analyze how the ideologies, sensibilities, and understandings of the *9/11 project* permeate and inform these films and the messages they deliver in relation to race, gender, sexuality, and what it means to be an American citizen in the 9/11 world.

Finally, writing about 9/11 issues and ideologies implies a discrete time frame. However, as a time period, 9/11 has a definitive start in 2001 but no clear end. We contend that while the election of Barack Obama in 2008, and his reelection in 2012, marked a conclusion to the 9/11 G. W. Bush era, much of the ideology developed after September 11, 2001, has survived the Bush administration itself (Bloodsworth-Lugo and Lugo-Lugo 2010). We keep with Kuznick and Gilbert's discussion of the Cold War, here, and their insight that Cold War ideology did not end with the Cold War itself but has extended well beyond that time (Bloodsworth-Lugo and Lugo-Lugo 2010, 11). In addition, other events have helped fashion the historical moment that might be called 9/11 and shaped the American lens after September 11, 2001. Most noteworthy, in this regard, has been the recent economic crisis, or Great Recession, and we dedicate a chapter to this discussion. Mainly, we argue that the specter of 9/11 carries so much weight that even the Great Recession was framed using "us versus them" discourse and advanced a 9/11 ideology. With this in mind, we treat films released after the election of Barack Obama, as well as films featuring the economic crisis, as 9/11 films. This includes, for instance, *Wall Street: Money Never Sleeps* (Oliver Stone, 2010)—a sequel to a much earlier film, *Wall Street* (Oliver Stone, 1987). Because *Wall*

Street: Money Never Sleeps reflects the happenings and anxieties of 2010, however, it should be considered a self-standing film rather than a sequel to a 1980's film. We maintain that while it is important to situate 9/11 within a historical time frame, it is likewise crucial to understand 9/11 as an ongoing societal and cultural project—a project that both borrows from previous eras and informs our lives in specific, novel, and ongoing ways.

CHAPTER PROGRESSION

In chapter 2, "White Masculinity and the (In)Security of 9/11," we provide an analysis of three mainstream films that explicitly portray the events of September 11, 2001. Specifically, we consider *World Trade Center* (Oliver Stone, 2006), *United 93* (Paul Greengrass, 2006), and, more recently, *Extremely Loud & Incredibly Close* (Stephen Daldry, 2012), in order to identify and initiate a discussion of relevant themes from the *9/11 project* vis-à-vis constructions or productions of race, gender, sexuality, and citizenship. These films, with their clear and obvious connections to the events of September 11, 2001, present interesting examples, for even though they do not portray the infrastructure of the *9/11 project* (for it did not exist on September 11, 2001), they still portray the tropes and ideologies developed about that day. Because of this, these films serve as a primer for the analysis developed in subsequent chapters. In particular, we discuss representations of white maleness or white male American citizenship, as white men are threatened by terrorism and assume the role of protector within the protection/threat binary. We also explore the paradoxical adherence to, and performance of, white male American citizenship by central nonwhite and nonmale characters in these films. We see in these performances a demonstration necessary for accessing American citizenship, as it is constituted in a United States embracing the *9/11 project*.

In chapter 3, "War and Sexualized/Racialized Threats," we argue that the *9/11 project* has informed our collective imagination so thoroughly that depictions of soldiers, even mentally and/or physically damaged soldiers, become part of the narrative of "us vs. them." Thomas Pollard notes that movies after September 11, 2001, have marked "some of the most pessimistic, violent, and cynical movies of all time" (2009, 206). Jonathan Markovitz adds, "Hollywood has a long history of turning widespread fears into cinematic spectacles, but never before has the source of those fears been so singular, so easily isolated, or so thoroughly disseminated to national and international audiences" (2004, 201). Films are capable of showcasing our ideologies, and 9/11 films have featured a specific set of perceptions. Our concern in this chapter is with the way films embody, reflect, and portray a set of assumptions about U.S. culture at the start of the twenty-first century and specific ideological leanings of the United States during this time. Here, we focus on two war movies, *Home of the Brave* (Irwin Winkler, 2007) and *The Hurt Locker* (Kathryn Bigelow, 2009), to address the U.S. response of war to the events of September 11, 2001, including how ideologies developed after "the day that changed America" might be reconciled with notions of home and safety. We also discuss two nonwar movies, *V for Vendetta* (James McTeigue, 2006), which provides viewers with a fictitious non-American scenario, and *Avatar* (James Cameron, 2009), which depicts a literal out-of-this-world setting, as examples of the *9/11 project* interacting with and constructing race, sexuality, and citizenship in these imaginary settings. We highlight ways that viewers might be expected to read and engage with these themes, given the *9/11 project*.

In chapter 4, "Narratives of Threat and 9/11 Monsters," we argue that, similar to the last two films discussed in the previous chapter, a number of films develop the discourse and ideologies of 9/11 by creating allegories and without specifically addressing the events of September 11, 2001, themselves. By so doing, the films explore American anxieties in the wake of a changed America, including how Americans might respond to and ultimately cope with an increasing number of 9/11 monsters. In *Monsters to Destroy: The Neoconservative War on Terror and Sin*, Ira Chernus conveys:

> Tales of a battle between good and evil must depict the world as a threatening or even terrifying place, full of monsters. That alone would be enough to make people feel insecure. But there is more. The stories always imply (and often say quite openly) that the monsters can never be destroyed. (2006, 4–5)

We consider *Flight Plan* (Robert Schwentke, 2005), *The Brave One* (Neil Jordan, 2007), and *Lakeview Terrace* (Neil LaBute, 2008), which all clearly highlight threat and danger in a 9/11 world and the difficulty of suppressing and containing it. The main character in *The Brave One*, Erica Baine (Jodie Foster), describes New York as "an organism that changes, mutates." Erica is herself transformed in the wake of the loss of her fiancé, who is beaten to death as the couple takes a nighttime stroll and discusses plans for their wedding. Like the September 11, 2001, attacks on the city, the attack on the couple arrives "out of the blue," on a beautiful and otherwise normal day. In response, Erica devolves into a vigilante killer—now "fearing the place [she] once loved" and finding herself changed into a stranger (a stranger lurking inside all along). Erica discovers a monstrous inside in response to her encounter with a monstrous outside, as well as an uncertain future, with an expanding array of monsters to destroy.

Flight Plan and *Lakeview Terrace* both develop the notion of the stranger or enemy within, but in these films, that enemy becomes the person assigned to one's very security and protection—the air marshal and the police officer, respectively. This embodiment of the monster reveals no space as immune from danger in a 9/11 world, together with a greater required vigilance in both identifying and managing these times of uncertainty and the monsters that create it. In this chapter, we examine the racialized and gendered features of these messages and their portrayal in these films, including issues of borders and boundaries as they engage with 9/11 notions of American security and citizenship.

In chapter 5, "9/11 Transnationalism and Gendered Citizenship," we argue that the *9/11 project* (re)creates the world as an uncontained, frightening, and unpredictable space. The 9/11 filmic world tends to reveal no borders for First World peoples, while it maintains strict divisions for non-First World citizens. In fact, within this world, a person's citizenship becomes entangled with her/his gender and the space he or she inhabits. Ultimately, a person's place in the world becomes dichotomized in terms of salvation or damnation. We examine the films *Babel* (Alejandro Gonzalez Inarritu, 2006), *Children of Men* (Alfonso Cuaron, 2007), and *Eat Pray Love* (Ryan Murphy, 2010). *Babel* offers a broad account of the world after September 11, 2001, especially as Americans have conceived of it vis-à-vis issues of threat and containment, while centering citizenship and the global flow of goods and bodies. This film also portrays central elements of the infrastructure of the *9/11 project*. *Children of Men* presents a world without children—that is, a world without a future. This world is enveloped by chaos, and when the European protagonist finds an African pregnant woman, he resolves to save the species. *Eat Pray Love* tells the story of Liz (Julia Roberts), a white American woman using the world to save herself from herself by gaining a relevant insight. The fluidity of the world in *Eat Pray Love* serves as a backdrop to Liz's search for meaning, and her citizenship serves as her passport. All three films feature versions of 9/11 First World citizenship—one that is granted to white American and European bodies, and one that becomes useful for attempting to understand a newly revealed chaos. This kind of citizenship encounters trouble in the uncontained world; however, it overcomes obstacles and saves itself (and others) in the process.

In chapter 6, "Animated 9/11 Raciality and Conceptions of Progress," we suggest that several recent animated feature films employ notions of progress as primary motivators for their stories, effectively eliding matters of race and historical inequalities in the process. Presenting circumstances and desires as "human" and "universal," rather than as "white" and "Western" (or "American"), these films advance assumptions regarding what it means to move forward in a 9/11 era, which has paradoxically also been touted as a postracial era by social commentators (Adam Nagourney 2008; Daniel Schorr 2008). We contend that the notions of progress deployed in these films are both familiar (unfolding within a long human history) and unique (situated within a 9/11 United States). Animated films, far from being mere and innocent forms of entertainment, can be interpreted as "teaching machines," in the words of Henry Giroux (1999). As such, animated films "inspire at least as much cultural authority and legitimacy for teaching specific roles, values, and ideals [as] more traditional sites of learning" (quoted in King, Lugo-Lugo, and Bloodsworth-Lugo 2010, 8). In this chapter, we consider three recent animated films, *Planet 51* (Jorge Blanco, 2009), *The Princess and the Frog* (Ron Clements, 2009), and *Rio* (Carlos Saldanha, 2011), highlighting their 9/11 messages regarding progress. We argue that 9/11 lessons unfold within these films despite the particular contexts for their stories. *Planet 51* is set in another part of the galaxy, *The Princess and the Frog* is placed in 1920s New Orleans, and *Rio* is located in Rio de Janeiro, Brazil. Within these films, specific place and time become irrelevant, for they only serve as background to the deployment of 9/11 ideologies.

In chapter 7, "The Great Recession and White Masculine (In)security," we begin to conclude our analysis with Hollywood films that profile the recent global recession, and which, in turn, underscore 9/11 ideological notions of protection, security, and the containment of threats. We analyze *Up in the Air* (Jason Reitman, 2009), *The Company Men* (John Wells, 2011), *Wall Street: Money Never Sleeps* (2010), and *Larry Crowne* (Tom Hanks, 2011) to argue that white male American citizenship is revealed as under attack within these films as they engage with the Great Recession situated within a 9/11 framework. Similar to the films portraying the events of September 11, 2001, analyzed in chapter 2, the films included in this chapter create a narrative around white male American citizenship. In these films, this identity is depicted as being endangered and in need of reconstitution. As the tagline for *The Company Men* conveys, "In America, we give our lives to our jobs. It's time to take them back." This "taking back" can be read as a reclaiming of white male Americanness, as the economy marks a perceived threat to the quintessential representation of the American citizen—a citizen in need of that reclamation.

In chapter 8, "9/11 End-of-Days Hollywood," we specifically address the rhetoric unfolding through the *9/11 project*, which has led to specific ways of framing the world, and how this rhetoric has been portrayed in disaster or apocalyptic movies. Perceived threats to Americanness work to (re)construct race, gender, and citizen-ship, and these portrayals and workings can be considered through recent Hollywood films of various genres. We gesture to the recent popularity of zombie and "end of world" films to address anxieties over impending and catastrophic threats, failed preparations and management of threats, and white male attempts to contain and secure borders and boundaries. We briefly consider *Take Shelter* (Jeff Nichols, 2011), *Contagion* (Steven Soderbergh, 2011), and *World War Z* (Marc Forster, 2013). With these films, mainstream viewers are presented with danger in the form of an imagined or real storm, a novel and spreading disease, and a zombie pandemic. With taglines such as, "Don't talk to anyone. Don't touch anyone" (*Contagion*), and "Remember Philly!" (*World War Z*), end of world

9/11 films display danger as always anywhere and everywhere, as global. They show that strategies must be enacted in the face of a newly emerging and foreign world. While not explicitly referencing race, gender, and American citizenship, these films nonetheless offer 9/11 lessons through their filmic representations and underscoring of the *9/11 project* in an era after September 11, 2001.

Finally, we would like to address the title of the book, which uses a double entendre to situate the discussion of 9/11 films. On the one hand, *Projecting 9/11* refers to the process we have explained in detail in this chapter through which the *9/11 project* and 9/11 itself have come to life. On the other hand, the title also alludes to the process by which 9/11 is projected to viewers via the big screen. The two processes combined inform our efforts here.

Chapter Two

White Masculinity and the (In)Security of 9/11

A movie trailer has never made me cry. Until now. I watched the trailer for the upcoming film, *United 93*. I had to see for myself if it was as gut-wrenching as people are saying. I have the answer. Almost five years later, the trailer for this film evoked the same horror and sadness that the actual events did when I watched them unfold on September 11, 2001. I cried five years ago when two towers came crashing down and planes fell out of the sky. And I cried now as I watched the same events unfold again. Only this time, all of it was neatly packaged as part of a Hollywood production. But it was as real now as it was then. (Curth 2006)

Just prior to the ten-year anniversary of the September 11, 2001, events, a *USA Today*/Gallup poll revealed, "Ten years after the 9/11 terror attacks, 28% of Americans say they have permanently changed the way they live as a result of that tragedy" (Jones 2011). More than this, "58% believe that Americans overall have permanently changed the way they live" (Jones 2011). While it might be expected that Americans' perceptions of the effects of the events of September 11, 2001, on the country and on their lives, would lessen with the passage of time, the numbers from this poll show that this has not been the case, as a great percentage of those polled believed that "Americans' lives and their own lives have permanently changed" since that day.

The fact that this poll coincides with the ten-year anniversary of the September 11, 2001, events is of interest to us, given the notion that, as Karen Randell discusses in relation to national traumatic events, "audiences need at least 'ten years' in which to process the trauma of 9/11." She places this claim in historical context by noting that there "was not an *explicit* combat film made for seven years after the First World War and for thirteen years after the Vietnam War" (2010, 144–45). Randell maintains that this gap "is symptomatic of the cultural climate that exists after a national traumatic event and can also be understood in terms of the need for temporal space in which to assimilate its various traumas" (145). She points out, "Representations of that day have been repeatedly returned to . . . not through explicit narrative but through a referentiality that allows its audiences to assimilate events via mediated images, dialogues, and echoes of the attack" (145). Randell continues that this explains why there has been an "apparent void in production of the 9/11 narrative within the dominant Hollywood film form"; instead, there has been "a mediated return to a mediated event" (145–46). This is to say, according to the author, the events of September 11, 2001, have been referenced a multiplicity of times but hardly ever presented or portrayed by Hollywood to American audiences. We return to this point below. Relatedly, in a more in-depth set of questions, the same Gallup poll asked Americans about the extent to which September 11, 2001, had affected *them*. The questions were structured as follows: "As a result of the events that occurred on September 11, would you say that you are less willing to [INSERT ACTIVITY] or not?" According to the results, 24 percent of respondents were less willing to fly on airplanes; 20 percent were less willing to go into skyscrapers; 38 percent were less likely to travel overseas; and 27 percent were less likely to attend events where thousands of people are gathered (Jones 2011).

Another Gallup poll (2014), this one longitudinal, and conducted since 1995, sheds light on the impact of the events of September 11, 2001, on Americans. It asked Americans how worried they are that they or someone in their families would "become victims of terrorism." During the five years prior to the events of September 11, 2001, 24 to 42 percent responded that they were very or somewhat worried, with the year 2000 registering the lowest percentage (24 percent). From 2001 to 2013, 28 to 59 percent responded that they were very or somewhat worried. In those years, the responses fluctuated up and down, with the highest percentage (54 percent) registered in October 2001 and the lowest (28 percent) in 2004. Something to consider here is that the lowest percentage registered after September 11, 2001, is still higher than the lowest percentage before the events, showing that the events had a relatively long-lasting effect on Americans.

Former President G. W. Bush anticipated the long-term impact of the September 11, 2001, events on Americans in an Address to the Nation delivered on September 20, 2001, as he began to make a case for war. In his words:

> It is my hope that in the months and years ahead, life will return almost to [sic] normal. We'll go back to our lives and routines, and that is good. Even grief recedes with time and grace. But our resolve must not pass. Each of us will remember what happened that day, and to whom it happened. We'll remember the moment the news came—where we were and what we were doing. Some will remember an image of a fire, or a story of rescue. Some will carry memories of a face and a voice gone forever. (Bush 2001)

Approximately five years after September 11, 2001, major Hollywood studios released two films, each covering a main event of that day: *United 93* (2006) and *World Trade Center* (2006). In

April 2006, and in anticipation of these two films, Gallup asked Americans how likely it was that they would go to see these films. At the time, 60 percent said it was either not too likely or not likely at all that they would see them. Moreover, when Gallup asked whether they thought it was "a good or a bad thing for Hollywood to be making movies about the September 11th terrorist attacks," respondents were evenly split, with 44 percent saying it was a good thing and 44 percent saying it was a bad thing (Gallup 2014). Notably, these films are significant in that their return to September 11, 2001, is precisely *not* mediated; rather, the films hinge on and clearly depict the events of this day.

United 93 was released first and presented an account of the United Airlines flight that ultimately ended in a Pennsylvania field, after passengers reportedly struggled for control of the airplane in an attempt to stop terrorists from crashing it into another landmark. *World Trade Center*, on the other hand, detailed events at the World Trade Center Towers in New York City from the perspective of Port Authority police officers, some of whom were first responders trapped under rubble when the first tower collapsed. Given the films' different storylines, *United 93* portrays the last moments of passengers and crew members who died as heroes, while *World Trade Center* pays tribute to those who survived the attacks and helped save the lives of others. Embedded within the storylines and common to both films is a sense of national vulnerability and insecurity, played out through white and/or male lead characters. We use these two films as a primer for the discussion and analysis in subsequent chapters, for they were both released in the same year—the year marking the five-year anniversary of the September 11, 2001, events—and both provide a perfect example of Hollywood producers and directors using the *9/11 project* while looking back and depicting the same event that begot the project. As two of the first feature films depicting the events of that day, and as two films conceived and produced in the midst of an ongoing War on Terror, *United 93* and *World Trade Center* are clearly connected in their topics and depiction of events (again, using the project as a framework).

The issues in these films are carried forward in a ten-year 9/11-anniversary film, *Extremely Loud & Incredibly Close* (2012), in which a young boy's relationship to his father's death on September 11, 2001, parallels Americans' relationship to 9/11. The familiar and everyday is transformed into the unfamiliar and threatening, underscoring this relationship. A mark of the *9/11 project* is the perception that danger lurks everywhere—that no one can know when an everyday routine will turn tragic. The lack of certainty surrounding how to respond to such moments, and the feeling of vulnerability in the face of their enormity, characterizes the lessons of 9/11. This lack of certainty becomes a threat for Americans who, in the decade previous to September 11, 2001, had thrived on the assumption that nothing could harm their militarized empire. Importantly, it is the whiteness and maleness of both the perceived target of terrorism, and of those tasked with responding to terrorism, that typifies the 9/11 threat. We also explore the paradoxical adherence to, and performance of, white male American citizenship by central nonwhite and nonmale characters in these films. We claim that performances by nonwhite male characters provide a necessary condition for access to American citizenship, as it is constituted in the United States after September 11, 2001. White masculinity centers the narratives of these films, despite their plot differences, and frames 9/11 as a moment of national vulnerability and sacrifice.

UNITED 93:"LET'S ROLL" AND THE
SACRIFICE OF WHITENESS

Perhaps because of the difference in focus (death versus survival), and perhaps because *United 93* was released four months prior to

World Trade Center, moviegoers expressed strong reactions against *United 93* when trailers of the film first appeared in theaters during the spring of 2006. News outlets instantly reported people crying, shouting "too soon," and complaining to theater manage-ment that they were being forced to relive the events of September 11, 2001, through images in the trailer (Martelle 2006; Markert 2011). Richard Corliss (2006) describes the feedback as follows:

> Audiences who wouldn't flinch at slasher movies and serial-killer thrillers have shouted back at the previews. Some were angry, some in tears. They felt violated to see, in the guise of entertainment, a pinprick reminder of a tragedy for which Americans still grieve and which they may wish to keep buried, along with the people and the image of national invulnerability lost that day. Yet the events of 9/11, like a nightmare that haunts the waking, have permeated the media. Not just the all-news channels but also books, plays, songs.

While the last two sentences of Corliss's account are accurate in their assessment that the events of September 11, 2001, had been present in the lives of Americans through other media, the strong reactions to the trailer of a Hollywood feature film convey that movies are perhaps held to a different standard. Viewer complaints were so strong that an AMC theater in New York City pulled the trailer from its outlets (Martelle 2006; Neuman and Keegan 2006). Personal narratives of the experience of watching the trailer began to appear, as illustrated by the account of Traci Curth which opens this chapter. A mother of one of the passengers who died aboard the United airplane, Alice Hoagland, responded to claims that it was too soon for the film to be released: "I hope we're not as a society inured to the messages of the movie. I know it's not too soon. I hope it's not too late" (Corliss 2006).

United 93 was "dedicated to the memory of all those who lost their lives on September 11, 2001" (IMDb 2012). It was also deemed, by *Entertainment Weekly*, "one of the most controversial movies ever made" (Bierly et al. 2006). Directly addressing the controversy over the release of his film, director Paul Greengrass commented, "Movies need to address the way the world is. We have to tell stories about 9/11" (IMDb 2012). As we laid out in chapter 1 of this book, it is not really a matter of how the world *is* as much as of how we perceive it to be. Thus, in his film, Greengrass offers his recreation or perception of the events aboard United Airlines Flight 93, scheduled from Newark to San Francisco on September 11, 2001, which ultimately crashed in a Pennsylvania field. He uses a combination of actors to portray the passengers and the hijackers, and real-life flight attendants, pilots, air traffic controllers, and military personnel (in fact, some of the nonactors played themselves). On the making of *United 93*, Clayton Neuman and Rebecca Winters Keegan (2006) write:

> On a set in suburban London's Pinewood Studios, where many James Bond fantasies have been filmed, Greengrass staged this real-life, high-stakes death battle over and over—the whole ordeal, nonstop, in takes lasting from 20 to 55 min[utes], as the reconstructed Boeing 757 would wobble and shudder, and the camera crew followed the action like nosy paparazzi. Says Cheyenne Jackson, who plays Mark Bingham, one of the stalwart passengers: "We spent so many hours throwing our trays around and bleeding and screaming and crying and praying, and throwing up and peeing ourselves, and trying to imagine every possibility of what these people were going through. It was an environment where we could go to these deep, dark places. But the saddest thing about it was that finally we could wash off our makeup and come out of those places."

While viewers will never know the (actual) dark places encountered by the passengers of United Flight 93, as they dealt with the untenable situation of being aboard a hijacked and doomed aircraft, *United 93* conveys what U.S. mainstream viewers perceive they went through—a perception informed by the *9/11 project*.

Unlike most disaster films, which typically begin with shots of victims' daily and quiet routines, *United 93* begins with Arabic prayer and shots of the hijackers as they prepare themselves at a hotel. The sound of airplanes flying above offers a clear foreshadowing of what will come. The film does eventually move to the quotidian aspects of passengers waiting at their gates and boarding their planes, with air controllers performing their jobs. But interwoven with everyday moments are painful reminders of the unprecedented events that will eventually unfold. One such reminder occurs when, after being informed of noneventful atmospheric conditions across the country, the FAA national operations manager tells those working at the command center, "It'll be a good day in the East Coast." Another takes place a few minutes later when the pilot and head flight attendant agree on a "secret knock" before closing the cockpit door. The pilot tells her to do a "three one," and she rehearses it: three knocks in a row, followed by a single knock (as in three airplanes that hit their targets, followed by one that did not). A third reminder is seen when the pilot talks to passengers before departing and assures them that their prompt departure will put them at the gate in San Francisco "on time or a little bit early." And a final reminder happens once United Flight 93 is in the air. The pilot tells the passengers to look at "the nice view of New York's skyline." The passengers, as well as film viewers, get a glimpse of the Twin Towers still intact.

Since viewers know not only what will happen to the passengers on the plane, but also how and why, the importance of *United 93* lies not in what occurs as such, but in the story that is (re)created about what happens—the story that viewers are told. In fact, the narrative of *United 93* is very similar to that of *World Trade Center*, as we discuss in the next section, in that it revolves around whiteness, maleness, and citizenship. While it is clear from watching these films that white American men were not exclusively impacted by the events of September 11, 2001, it is nonetheless these men in which the vulnerability of the nation on that day is reflected. Viewers get a sense of these men from the start, as the predominantly white male cast is presented: passengers at the gate, air controllers, the pilot, and the commander in charge at the Northeast Air Defense Command Center (NEADS)—all of whom will be affected by, forced to manage, and faced with responding to the happenings and mounting frustrations of that day. The gathering of whiteness, maleness, and Americanness into one category is shorn up in the film when one of the air traffic controllers (a white American man) first identifies that there is a problem. In his words, "I heard some verbiage over the background. It was not American. It was foreign." This moment marks the definitive line separating American from non-American, as the English language is invoked as the quintessential marker for Americanness.

As the film advances, viewers begin to experience frustration as air controllers make repeated calls to various airplanes and get no response. Although the first third of the film is spent gathering a collective picture of these white American men, it also presents a full-scale destabilizing of the category once the second airplane hits the towers. This second hit is received in the film with approximately six seconds of silence. We see the (mostly) white men at the command center, the ones at an air control tower, and those at NEADS looking at their television screens in disbelief and horror. With the attack on the Pentagon, the FAA national operation's manager asks for a grounding of all planes and a suspension of incoming international flights. When a subordinate warns, "You are going to shut down the entire country right now," the operation's manager swiftly replies, "That's right. Listen, we're at war with someone and until we figure out what to do about it, we are shutting down. That's it. We are finished." Viewers also see the commander at NEADS repeatedly asking for permission to engage with the hijacked planes. He is told that only the president can give such permission, leading to a series of questions about the location of the president.

Viewers are almost able to experience, alongside these men, the gathering frustration of not being able to act, of not being able to communicate with or engage the hijacked planes and needing to "shut down" the country. It is uncomfortable to hear them ask questions such as, "How can a plane run into a tower like that?" and "What is going on?" Viewers know very well what is happening, and perhaps more importantly, they know precisely what will come next. The lack of action on the ground is juxtaposed to the action of the men in the air, as the all-white male passengers of United 93 organize to take over the airplane. The passengers' engagement is punctuated by the words of one of those men, who, just as they are about to "take matters into their own hands," urges the others by saying, "Are you guys ready? Let's roll, come on, let's go already." Of course, viewers also know that their actions will come too late, contributing to feelings of frustration and insecurity.

United 93 also uses communication technology to convey happenings of the day. Viewers are presented with a seeming overabundance of cell phones, especially for the time period, primarily being used by white men talking business. One of the hijackers uses his cell phone to communicate with a loved one (a good-bye call, viewers are to assume). But the most pressing aspect of communication technologies and white American men unfolds on the plane itself, since it is the white men who discover what has happened in New York City and at the Pentagon, using cell phones or air phones. Communication itself becomes a component in the fate of United Airlines Flight 93, as viewers learn at the end of the film that "military commanders were not notified that United 93 had been hijacked until four minutes after it had crashed." The devastation of this statement is most significant when viewers realize its implications: These white American men were struggling against the terrorists by themselves—alone. This sense of aloneness, underscoring the insecurity of 9/11, also emerges in *World Trade Center*.

WORLD TRADE CENTER:"THIS COUNTRY IS AT WAR" AND LESSONS OF 9/11

As with *United 93*, sociologist John Markert conveys that with *World Trade Center* there was an initial concern "over whether it was too soon or appropriate to graphically depict what happened" (2011, 40). However, the reception to this movie, as its trailer underwent a national rollout, differed from that of *United 93*. Film critic Eugene Novikov (2006) remarks, "If it was 'too soon' for *United 93*, it is assuredly not too soon for *World Trade Center*. It's a strong film, and a trailblazer for further cinematic efforts to explore September 11th and its aftermath."

World Trade Center takes viewers back, not only to the date of September 11, 2001, but to the place known as Ground Zero. Although everyone in the film is an actor, director Oliver Stone, similar to *United 93*'s Greengrass, uses "accounts of the surviving participants" to create the film (IMDb 2012). Like *United 93*, *World Trade Center* presents a story of white American maleness, and as with other disaster films, *World Trade Center* begins with intermittent shots of the early morning routines of the two main characters, Port Authority officers John McLoughlin (Nicolas Cage) and Will Jimeno (Michael Peña). Viewers see shots of the city and everyday activities: people waking, showering, driving, listening to the radio, discussing baseball on a full morning train, and a person walking their dog.

Once the first tower is hit, by what viewers already know is a hijacked airplane, the Port Authority Police Department is mobilized. With it, the film's two main characters and several of their colleagues are taken to what will be Ground Zero. On the way,

McLoughlin and his commanding officer (Charles Gargano) have the following exchange:

Commander: What special equipment we got down there?

[McLoughlin shakes his head.]

Commander: What?

McLoughlin: We prepared for everything. Car bombs, chemical, biological, an attack from the top. But not this. Not for something this size. There's no plan. We didn't make it.

As the officers arrive, they enter Tower One in an effort to help the evacuation process. The time between the strike of the first plane and the collapse of Tower One (onto the officers) is difficult to watch, as it is apparent they have no idea what is happening and are acting on misinformation. For instance, while on his cell phone on their way to "the city," Officer Pezzulo (Jay Hernandez) tells the others, "My wife says a second plane hit the other tower," to which a colleague responds, "Nah, that's just the smoke from the other tower." Once they are inside Tower One, they connect with Officer Amoroso (Jon Bernthal), a colleague from another precinct, who tells them that Tower Two is also in flames. When McLoughlin responds that it "must have caught fire from Tower One," Officer Amoroso responds, "I heard it was also hit." McLoughlin ends the conversation by saying, "No, Fields just said one plane, Tower One." A short while later, Officer Amoroso continues, "You guys hear about the Pentagon? It got hit. A missile or something. And Israel? It's gone. It's nuked." He concludes his narrative with, "The whole freaking world is coming to an end." This expression and sense that the world is ending is significant as a number of 9/11 feature films examine end-of-world scenarios that can be linked to 9/11 anxiety and insecurity. We return to some of these films in our concluding chapter.

Similar to the misinformation that unfolds in *United 93*, the misinformation in *World Trade Center* serves to underscore the unpreparedness of the men responding—and thus of the country's unpreparedness—to handle such an unprecedented situation. The situation's magnitude, for which McLoughlin acknowledges no existing plan (as well as knowing very few details of the unfolding day), is also highlighted by news reports throughout the film. During one such report, the newscaster states, "Officials seem simply stunned by the scale of the losses." The film's main characters spend most of their time in the film buried under rubble from Tower One. Once freed from the rubble, Jimeno asks, "Hey, where did the buildings go? Where did the buildings go?" A firefighter responds, "They are gone, kid," again underscoring the sheer magnitude of the day's happenings.

In addition to *World Trade Center*'s two main characters, an important figure in the film is Marine Staff Sergeant Dave Karnes (Michael Shannon), who is the only character to infer our future as a country from the events of the day. He proclaims to his coworkers, " I don't think you guys know this, but this country is at war." After telling his church pastor that God is calling on him to help, he heads from Ohio to New York City. When Karnes arrives, dressed in his full marine uniform, one of his first statements to a firefighter, after looking around at the lingering smoke, is this: " It's like God made a curtain with the smoke, shielding us from what we're not yet ready to see." Karnes and Sergeant Thomas (Marine Mapother), another marine at Ground Zero, decide to look for survivors under the rubble. The two men end up finding and helping to rescue Jimeno and McLoughlin. Afterwards, Karnes is seen speaking on his phone. While viewers only hear his side of the conversation, it is clear that he is talking to his employer. Karnes relays, "No, I'm not coming in today. . . . I don't know. . . . They are going to need some good men out there to avenge this . . . we'll see."

Near the end of the film, viewers learn that Jimeno and McLoughlin were numbers eighteen and nineteen, out of the twenty people found alive under the rubble. As a result of their injuries, they underwent multiple surgeries and months of rehabilitation. Before ending, the film fast-forwards two years, where viewers encounter a reunion. The two men arrive with their families, and a voice-over runs in which McLoughlin reflects on the events of September 11, 2001:

> 9/11 showed us what human beings are capable of. The evil, yeah, sure. But it also brought out a goodness we forgot could exist. People taking care of each other for no other reason than it was the right thing to do. It's important for us to talk about that good. To remember. 'Cause I saw all of it that day.

This narration conveys a great deal about how the director, and to an extent Americans in general, were reflecting upon the meaning of 9/11—attempting to come to terms with it and reconcile the events of September 11, 2001, by turning inward. However, in this looking back and looking within, viewers learn how Americans were seeing themselves in relation to 9/11. The fact that it is McLoughlin and *not* Jimeno, or McLoughlin *and* Jimeno, offering viewers his/their impressions of 9/11 highlights the whiteness of those procuring its lessons. McLoughlin's statement that it is "important for us to talk about that good" should raise questions concerning who is included in this "us." We address these issues more fully in the sections that follow.

EXTREMELY LOUD & INCREDIBLY CLOSE: THE PAIN "AT 9/11"

Ten years after September 11, 2001, Paramount Pictures released *Extremely Loud & Incredibly Close*. The film is set in 2002 and employs repeated flashbacks to September 11, 2001, and before. It presents viewers with Oskar Schell (Thomas Horn), a nine-year-old boy trying to keep alive his connection with his dead father, Thomas Schell (Tom Hanks). Thomas had a meeting at the World Trade Center Towers the morning of September 11, 2001, and he died in the attacks there. Oskar is portrayed as an incredibly bright but socially awkward child, having received inconclusive test results for Asperger autism. Through Oskar, viewers receive messages about coming to terms with 9/11—all through this young white American boy.

Throughout *Extremely Loud & Incredibly Close*, Oskar refers to September 11, 2001, as "the worst day." He repeats several times that his father "died at 9/11," turning a day into a quasi-tangible space. By way of the film's flashbacks, viewers learn that Thomas was an adoring father who tried to help his son, catering to his interests in science and exploration. The father and son played a game called "reconnaissance expedition," in which Thomas left clues for Oskar in an attempt to help him solve a problem. As part of the game, Oskar had to interact with people, which, as we hear Thomas tell Oskar's mother, Linda Schell (Sandra Bullock), "he has a hard time doing." At the time of Thomas's death, father and son were in the midst of playing "reconnaissance expedition number 6." In this particular game, Oskar was to determine whether New York City had a sixth borough, which Thomas describes as having previously existed, but that just "floated away"—much as part of Manhattan would "float away" with the events of September 11, 2001, taking Oskar's father along with it.

As Oskar grieves for his father, he shatters a blue vase and finds a key in an envelope labeled "Black." He decides to track every person named "Black" in New York City to find the lock the key opens. Oskar conveys, "I started with a simple problem: a key with no lock." As he begins his journey, we learn that certain things make Oskar "panicky." With the events of "the worst day," his list of panic-inducing objects has expanded:

> Old people, running people, airplanes, tall things, things you can
> get stuck in, loud things, screaming, crying, people with bad
> teeth, bags without owners, shoes without owners, children
> without parents, ringing things, smoking things, people eating
> meat, people looking up, towers, tunnels, speeding things, loud
> things [he lists "loud things" twice], things with lights, things
> with wings, and bridges. Bridges make me especially panicky.

Even before September 11, 2001, but especially afterward, Oskar is concerned about things not being safe. He rattles a tambourine, for comfort, as he walks.

Prior to learning about Oskar's panic, viewers see that he has bought a new answering machine. It is identical to one owned by his parents, and he switches the two. By this point in the film, viewers have heard two messages left on the old machine, both from his father. The first message says that something is happening and they are telling people to stay put and wait for firemen; the second message conveys that things are "a bit chaotic." Viewers are not privy to the other messages, but they can see that the machine contains six messages in total. Importantly, Oskar keeps the messages a secret from his mother. He even lies to her when she asks whether his father has called. Later in the film, viewers learn that Thomas had contacted Linda to tell her that he was in a meeting on the 106th floor of the World Trade Center. He was still there when the building collapsed.

Oskar's quest to find the lock for the key is full of numbers and calculations, which viewers know have helped him to solve the mysteries of previous reconnaissance expeditions. Along with his father, these numbers and calculations have provided order and a sense of security in Oskar's life. It is obvious that the numbers did not keep him—or certainly, did not keep his father—safe "at 9/11." In his father's absence, it is Oskar's self-muted grandfather (Max von Sydow), whom Oskar is not supposed to know is his grandfather, who provides a sense of kinship. In Oskar's words, "Even though he never said a word, for the first time since Dad died, I felt like I had someone to talk to."

Significantly, Oskar's quest keeps his mother in the background until the very end of the film. In an earlier exchange, Oscar conveys that it does not make sense that they buried an empty box (referring to the burial held for his father), and Linda responds that many things do not make sense. In desperation, she yells, "It's never going to make sense, because it doesn't! I don't know why a man flew a plane into a building! I don't know why my husband is dead!" Oskar concludes the exchange by telling his mother, "I wish it were you. I wish it were you in the building that day." She responds, calmly, "Me too." When Oskar immediately apologizes, telling her that he did not mean what he said, she replies, "Yes, you did."

We can ask why this boy is chosen to tell a story about 9/11. Perhaps an "average" child or person would have been too simple—unable to articulate 9/11 lessons. Here, we have a child who is different, special, with above-average intelligence, always looking for clues and explanations about mysteries. Oskar is driving the quest for answers—the need to understand. He is very good with numbers, facts, and science; yet, he remains lost in his search for answers about his father and about 9/11. Perhaps this makes it all right for viewers to feel lost about the meaning of 9/11 as well. After all, if a child-genius is not able to understand 9/11, how can everyday viewers be expected to understand?

CONCLUSION

In *Extremely Loud & Incredibly Close*, Oskar only begins to make sense of 9/11 and his father's death when he meets William Black (Jeffrey Wright), a black man, and the owner of the key in Oskar's possession. William is the husband of Abbey Black (Viola Davis), the first person Oskar had interviewed in his search for the key's owner. Toward the end of the film, Abbey figures out that it is William whom Oskar must meet. And in the encounter between the child and the man, Oskar learns an important lesson: A key might open a lock, but it might not always solve a problem. He learns that the key is William's, left by *his* father, and that whatever it opens is for *William* to discover. Thomas had bought the blue vase from William at an estate sale after William's father had died, with the key accidentally left inside. Oskar finding the key was merely coincidental. Perhaps without realizing it, Oskar exchanges the key for a verbalization of what has been bothering him—the story of his father's sixth message.

Oskar admits to William that when his father called the final time, he (Oskar) was actually at the apartment but could not make himself answer the phone. Oskar states, "He needed me and I couldn't pick it up. He said, 'Are you there?' He could have said 'Is anyone there?' But I think he knew. I think he knew I was there and wanted to give me time to be brave enough to answer." According to Oskar, his dad asked the question "Are you there?" nine times. Viewers see it replayed. After the ninth time, the line goes dead. Viewers see Oskar look at the television screen as the tower collapses. In the final exchange between Oskar and William, viewers realize the significance of their meeting:

Oskar: Do you forgive me?

William: For not picking up?

Oskar: For not being able to tell anyone.

William: Of course I forgive you.

Oskar: I can't tell you how much better that makes me feel.

William's forgiveness provides a sort of redemption for Oskar. It may also serve as a form of forgiveness for all of us—stuck to our television screens on September 11, 2001, unable to say anything, unable to do anything. Oskar had not told anyone about the sixth message, including his mother. His mother never had the opportunity to hear *any* of the messages. While Oskar is able to form a sort of connection with his mother at the end of the film, it is only after she proves herself capable of speaking to Oskar in his "language" of numbers and calculations. "I thought only Dad could think like me," he quips. Even after this connection, and even after she tells him that what she misses most about her husband is his voice, Oskar does not share the messages his father left on the machine. In the end, it is only Oskar and his grandfather who receive that kind of resolution, with William serving a role of redemption for Oskar.

Returning to the films discussed earlier, *United 93* and *World Trade Center*, viewers see that the most prominent man of color in *United 93* is the African American copilot, First Officer LeRoy Homer (Gary Commock), who tells the pilot that he and his wife are planning to take a vacation in London and arrives at the wrong conclusion when first informed that two airplanes had hit the Twin Towers—"must have been student pilots." In *World Trade Center*, the most obvious man of color is Will Jimeno. However, Jimeno is never racially identified in the film. The real-life Jimeno is of Colombian descent and is played by Mexican American actor Michael Peña. The character appears to embody the "Latino" stereotype typically presented by Hollywood, and viewers can assume that he is Latino. But other than his physical appearance, there is nothing "ethnic" or racially marked about him. In fact, he listens to country music. He also approves of the name Donna (McLoughlin's wife's name) by telling him, "That's a good name. It's real American, you know?" And he identifies his own wife, Allison (Maggie Gyllenhaal), as Italian and German. Jimeno has one daughter named Bianca, which means white in Italian. And along with Olive and Alyssa, the names being considered by Jimeno and his pregnant wife for their unborn second daughter, the children are placed closer to their Italian mother than their Latino father.

We are not suggesting that the copilot's plan to vacation in London with his wife or Jimeno's love of country music *make* these characters white, but these markers certainly make white audiences comfortable, and they place the characters within the established white narrative. Ultimately, they are portrayed as honorary whites. As such, these men of color have been given a "whitened sensibility" for the comfort of American viewers, who, like the films' producers and directors, perceive 9/11 as an experience primarily relevant to white Americans and, more specifically, to white American men. In fact, "white" is the implied modifier of "American" in the description of the term "us" used at the end of *World Trade Center*, referring to those who should heed the lessons of this day. The fewer cues about nonwhites and nonwhiteness produced by these films, the more comfortable mainstream American viewers will be about the characters, the films, and their own relationship to 9/11. Reinforcing that comfort is the fact that roles for men of color in these three films follow classic archetypes: a black character offering closure or redemption for a white character (William Black), a nearly invisible and barely-there black character (LeRoy Homer), and a racialized Latino in a supporting role to a white character (Will Jimenez).

Moreover, with *World Trade Center*, it becomes clear that American filmmakers and American viewers could not envision a nonwhite response to the attacks of September 11, 2001. As trailers for the film were being released, it became public that Sergeant Thomas, the marine who joins Sergeant Karnes in the search for survivors at Ground Zero, is a black American man. However, in the film's depiction of this real-life figure, Thomas is portrayed by William Mapother, a white actor (Associated Press 2006; Todd 2006). According to journalist Deborah Todd, *World Trade Center* producer Michael Shamberg stated that he knew about Sergeant

Thomas's role in the rescue but was unable to find him when creating the film (2006). Shamberg conveyed that producers did not discover Thomas was a black man until after they had begun shooting. He also said that despite the fact that McLoughlin cowrote the film, and Jimeno was consulted for authenticity, no one ever asked them for a physical description of Thomas. The importance of this fact is not so much that a white actor played Thomas but that no one in the film's production team even envisioned a nonwhite marine assisting in the rescue efforts on September 11, 2001. They did not ask for physical characteristics because they thought they knew what a 9/11 rescuer and hero looked like: white and male—that is, quintessentially American.

Chapter Three

War and Sexualized/Racialized Threats

> It was cinema, and popular culture in general, that, more than anything else, helped cast the disturbing events of 9/11, and the even more disturbing events that followed, into an easily accessible, easily digestible story, one in which everyone had a role to play, as either hero or villain, good or evil, "with us" or against us. (Aslan 2010, xii)

The wars in Afghanistan and Iraq were promoted by the G. W. Bush administration as components of the global and ongoing War on Terror. However, among Americans, a dissonance of feelings toward these efforts can be seen. In 2013, 53 percent of Americans considered the Iraq war to be a mistake, while 51 percent reported the same about the war in Afghanistan (Dugan 2013). The slight difference in percentages might be partially explained by the fact that Americans have tended to see the war in Iraq as a separate military action from the War on Terror, while they have considered the war in Afghanistan to be an aspect of the War on Terror (Dugan 2013). It makes sense, then, that Americans would generally support the war in Afghanistan insofar as they have supported the War on Terror. And they have. In 2007, 52 percent of Americans were very or somewhat satisfied with "the way things are going for the U.S." and 60 percent thought things were going very or somewhat well with the War on Terror (Gallup 2014). However, regardless of some inconsistencies in how Americans have felt toward war efforts, their feelings toward soldiers, especially soldiers who have participated in these efforts, are quite clear. In 2007 a Gallup poll showed that 81 percent of Americans thought "government leaders pay too little attention to the needs of military veterans" (Jones 2007).

The up and down nature of these polls reflects, we argue, not erratic messaging but difficulties faced by the Bush and Obama administrations when trying to reconcile the ideologies of the *9/11 project* with the reality of war—one of the more brutal aspects of its infrastructure. The first two films we discuss in this chapter bring this dissonance to the fore by portraying soldiers returning to the United States from war zones in Iraq and their struggles to return to "normal." This scenario reveals a major flaw in the infrastructure of the *9/11 project* as well as Hollywood's portrayal of the discrepancies shown by the polls. The second two films analyzed in this chapter are not about war efforts or the 9/11 infrastructure at all; rather, they position themselves within fantastical warlike scenarios to reference key ideological aspects of the *9/11 project*, including the 9/11 white racial and gendered frame. In their totality, the films provide viewers with both literal and metaphorical deployments of the *9/11 project*.

We would like to revisit Turner's (2006) notion that film is a source of significance for viewers, and our assertion that, instead of being forceful substitutes of reality, films are ideological representations at a given time based on cultural perceptions of reality. As sources of meaning and potential influential perceptions of reality, films hold a key to comprehending the culture and time in which they are created. In this chapter, we argue that Hollywood mainstream films have become, perhaps, the most pervasive medium by which conceptions of America and Americanness have been systematically rearticulated in a 9/11 era. Building upon our analysis in chapter 2, we claim that these reconceptions have transpired within the 9/11 white racial and gendered frame—a framework that sometimes includes perceived sexualized and racialized threats to white male citizenship. In the case of the films analyzed here, these threats are all embedded within narratives and ideologies involving war.

In his essay "Hollywood 9/11: Time of Crisis," Pollard conveys that as the events of September 11, 2001, unfolded, "no one could have predicted Hollywood's eventual reaction to these events," and producers "suspended many productions" because they were "fearful of offending a public shocked and in mourning for the attack's victims" (2009, 195). Pollard continues, "Months later it seemed to be business as usual [in Hollywood]" (195). Hollywood's initial reaction to halt many productions for fear that viewers might be offended was not unfounded, as demonstrated by responses to the *United 93* trailer five years after September 11, 2001, discussed in the previous chapter. According to Wheeler W. Dixon, 9/11 films reflect a "variety of impulses; some films seem to encourage the warrior spirit, while others question it, and others still avoid the issue altogether" (2004, 1). For our purposes, whether films produced and released after September 11, 2001, encourage the warrior spirit is not as important as whether they embody, reflect, and portray a set of assumptions about U.S. culture at the beginning of the twenty-first century, including what they can teach us about the ideological leanings of U.S. society during this time—that is to say, how they portray the ideological components of the *9/11 project*.

Different from the films discussed in chapter 2, the films addressed here are not specifically *about* the events of September 11, 2001. However, they do depict the structural aftermath of that fateful day, as well as the ideologies that crystallized around it, including rhetorical strategies concerning race, gender, sexuality, and citizenship. Two films deal with war and its effect on soldiers (*Home of the Brave* and *The Hurt Locker*); the other two, while seemingly unrelated to September 11, 2001, reveal a deep immersion in 9/11 cultural and ideological production (*V for Vendetta* and *Avatar*). Both types of film suggest a reexamination of Americanness in a 9/11 era and 9/11 influences on U.S. society and culture. In the view of Jeffrey Melnick, the films portray a decidedly 9/11 sensibility by combining the elements of war efforts, fears, anxieties, and perceptions specifically developed in the aftermath of the September 11, 2001, events. These elements form the core of 9/11 constructions of race, gender, sexuality, and citizenship. In what follows, we highlight the tropes activated within these films and how viewers might read and engage with them, highlighting central aspects of the *9/11 project*.

THE CONFLICT WITHIN AND WHITE MASCULINITY

Rebecca Bell-Metereau argues, "American blockbuster movies laid the groundwork for the public's response to [September 11, 2001] as the beginning of war rather than as a terrorist attack" (2004, 143–44). In our view, the groundwork for transforming September 11, 2001, into an act of war was laid by the rhetoric developed by the G. W. Bush administration, which consistently articulated the events of that day as an act of war (Bloodsworth-Lugo and Lugo-Lugo 2010; Snauwaert 2004). We can see this as early as nine days after the attacks, in his address to Congress, when President Bush stated:

> On September the 11th, enemies of freedom committed an act of war against our country. Americans have known wars—but for the past 136 years, they have been wars on foreign soil, except for one Sunday in 1941. Americans have known the casualties of war—but not at the center of a great city on a peaceful morning. Americans have known surprise attacks—but never before on thousands of civilians. All of this was brought upon us in a single day—and night fell on a different world, a world where freedom itself is under attack. (Bush 2001)

Within this short passage, the president used the word "war" four times. He also began his 2002 State of the Union address with the following words, "As we gather here today, our nation is at war" (Bush 2002a). In his 2003 State of the Union address, he referred to "this global war against a scattered network of killers" (Bush 2003). He continued, "The war goes on, and we are winning" (Bush 2003). Finally, in the 2004 State of the Union address, the last address delivered before his reelection, President Bush clearly stated, "Inside the United States, where the war began, we must continue to give homeland security and law enforcement personnel every tool they need to defend us" (Bush 2004).

These are just a few examples of primary speeches given by the former president in which he alluded to the United States being in a state of war. While we would like to emphasize presidential rhetoric as establishing the foundation for construing the events of September 11, 2001, as acts of war, we do not disagree that Hollywood feature films (blockbusters or not) further promoted this conception. Specifically, we propose that Hollywood movies crystallized the president's rhetorical message, making "war speak" more ordinary and placing it into the collective mainstream vocabulary and consciousness. Terms such as "collateral damage," "enemy combatant," "roadside bomb," "rendition," "troops," and "deployment" are a few examples.

Mainstream war movies and films with war speak and sensibilities have helped shape 9/11 ideologies concerning the world in which we now live and have offered common themes framing a 9/11 U.S. culture. Two of the more clearly present themes, addressed below, include the idea that with September 11, 2001, war came to our shores and is within us/our borders, as well as the notion that since that day we live in a different America and different world. The president's words cited above, "Inside the United States, where the war began," are of utmost importance for the first point (Bush 2004). His words, "We are living in a great time of change," and

"Those of us who have lived through these challenging times have been changed by them," illustrate the second point (Bush 2002a). Below, we examine *The Home of the Brave* (2007) and *The Hurt Locker* (2009) to outline how these two themes have played out and interacted in 9/11 films about war and war efforts.

Clearly influenced by the G. W. Bush administration's articulation of 9/11 as an act of war on U.S. soil, and perhaps influenced by what appears to be a dissonance of thinking among Americans vis-à-vis war efforts, Hollywood filmmakers have translated the September 11, 2001, attacks and ensuing War on Terror as a disruption or alteration of daily life within the United States—one in need of resolution or repair. A place once deemed safe is no longer safe, as the American public has endured a national trauma. Within 9/11 war movies, soldiers are featured as main characters commonly struggling with their return to the United States and a sense of normalcy. In addition to *Home of the Brave* and *The Hurt Locker*, examples of such films include *The Lucky Ones* (Neil Burger, 2008), *Stop-Loss* (Kimberly Pierce, 2008), and *Brothers* (Jim Sheridan, 2009). Soldiers in these films suffer from anxiety, flashbacks, nightmares, insomnia, numbness, and depression, as well as detachment and isolation from family members and friends. While these displays of behavior are recognized impacts of war on individuals, it is the message delivered to American viewers that interests us here. As a collective, Americans have been placed in a similar position to these individual soldiers insofar as they themselves have been grappling with a different America in the context of 9/11. The question of how this new America in turn shapes American citizens' perceptions of themselves and others, as well as ways in which the category "American" has been articulated and reimagined in the wake of the September 11, 2001, attacks, form central aspects of our work here.

HOME OF THE BRAVE AND *THE HURT LOCKER*: "GOING BACK" AND THE BURDEN OF 9/11

In *Home of the Brave*, the four main characters—a white woman and man, Vanessa Price (Jessica Biel) and Tommy Yates (Brian Presley), and two black men, Jamal Aiken (Curtis Jackson) and Dr. Will Marsh (Samuel L. Jackson)—experience dislocation when their company is sent home to Spokane, Washington, from Iraq. As discussed above, the four soldiers illustrate Americans' concerns that government officials are not paying enough attention to the needs of veterans. Having been caught in an ambush and roadside bombing, Price has lost her arm. When she returns home, viewers see her struggling with daily routines such as buttoning her shirt, folding the laundry, and putting items in her car. Aiken, unable to find solace in group therapy or to reconnect with his former girlfriend, shows a loss of hope and is killed in a shoot-out with police. Dr. Marsh, evidently troubled, turns to alcohol. However, it is in the character of Tommy Yates that viewers find a key to understanding the inner war of these soldiers and how their struggle might be extended more broadly to an American public still grappling with the effects of September 11, 2001, and the *9/11 project*.

Yates's best friend, Jordan (Chad Michael Murray), has died in the same ambush in which Price's arm has been severed. Price and Yates encounter each other in Spokane and share their impressions of returning home. They discuss similar trouble relating to others and have an extended conversation regarding their medications. The two agree that nothing is the same as before. As the film unfolds, Yates remains unable to find a place of comfort or belonging. In the film's final scene, entitled "Going Back," viewers see Price and Marsh finally resuming their lives in Spokane by way of a high school baseball game they attend with their families. Yates, on the other hand, is in the process of returning to Iraq. Viewers are offered a voice-over narration of a letter Yates has written to his parents regarding his decision to return:

Dear Mom and Dad:

I know you don't understand why I reenlisted. It's confusing
and scary for all of us. I know that. But I have to go back. I don't
want to die and Jordan didn't want to die, either. And maybe
when we went over there the first time we didn't know what we
were getting into. Maybe the leaders of our country didn't know
what they were getting into. Maybe the people don't want us
there, and maybe this whole thing is just making it worse. But
even after all that, I can't stay behind knowing that there are
soldiers over there getting attacked every day and dying every
day. I don't feel like it's wrong of me for wanting to go back
over there and help them. I'm going back. And I'm going back
to do the best job I know how and get back to you as soon as I
can. Pray for me.

Viewers do not learn whether Yates is able to resolve his sense
of displacement by returning to Iraq, but in the letter to his parents,
"going back" implies a source of redemption. Thus, viewers witness the white male vulnerability and insecurity that we discussed
in the previous chapter, which transforms into the white male burden attending the nation's response to September 11, 2001—specifically, in this case, the response of war. Yates reenlists not because
he believes he is fighting a just war (as he conveys, "maybe this
whole thing [war] is making it worse"), but because it provides the
only means he can see of managing his perceived responsibility.
Viewers are to assume that his decision offers a resolution not
available in Spokane, even if the outcome of that decision goes
unseen within the film. By extension, viewers are reassured of the
necessity of war overseas, given the new America emerging from a
war they have been told came to our shores on September 11, 2001,
but one that paradoxically cannot be resolved within these borders.

Significantly, the final scene of the film raises questions about
whether "going back" is ever really possible, thus complicating any
straightforward understanding of this phrase. In the cases of Price
and Marsh, returning to the life they had known was not feasible,

even if the baseball game offered a sort of homecoming (albeit to a home different from the one they had previously known). For Yates, returning to war was not fully "going back," as his return to Iraq was a year later, with a different group of soldiers, minus his best friend, and with the knowledge that a normal and routine life in Spokane was more difficult, in some ways, than one on the front lines. As mentioned above, Spokane could not house his responsibility or redemption.

Making a case for invading Iraq, President Bush stated, "The attacks of September 11th showed our country that vast oceans no longer protect us from danger" (Bush 2002b). And as referenced above, in his State of the Union address this same year, the president was clear that "our nation is at war," adding that "our economy is in recession, and the civilized world faces unprecedented dangers" (Bush 2002a). In an additional speech prior to signing the Homeland Security Act, he remarked, "With a vast nation to defend, we can neither predict nor prevent every conceivable attack. We're fighting a new kind of war against determined enemies" (Bush 2002c). These presidential messages were clear and consistent, conveying that there is a danger around us unlike any that has ever existed. This danger, in turn, characterizes a new and unpredictable world—one making new demands on Americans (especially white, male citizens) and bringing forth a new America.

Consequently, it is not surprising to envisage soldiers experiencing a profound sense of anxiety and displacement. We maintain that within Hollywood feature films, this displacement reflects a sense of unfamiliarity experienced by average Americans in the wake of the September 11, 2001, events—a sense of being thrown into unprecedented and fearful territory. In the face of this territory, Americans must develop a strong sense of responsibility—a responsibility that can, as in the case of Yates, transform into a burden. If we follow the logic of the rhetoric promoted by the G. W. Bush administration, soldiers are not returning to the same country.

The changes to their country are put into relief through the banality of daily life they experience. Viewers see this contradiction in *Home of the Brave* when Dr. Marsh tends to the grill in his backyard during a friendly get-together celebrating his homecoming. As his guests chat and laugh, viewers witness Marsh's removal from the party, his detachment from this everyday activity. Similarly, in *The Hurt Locker* (briefly discussed below), viewers see Sergeant William James (Jeremy Renner) walking through a cereal aisle with a vast array of choices. As he stands relatively paralyzed in the face of this aisle, its everydayness offers a stark contrast to the intensity of the bomb-defusing mission he had held in Iraq.

The Hurt Locker, like *Home of the Brave*, highlights war efforts after September 11, 2001. The film compares Sergeant James's seemingly nonchalant behavior while trying to diffuse multiple bombs in Iraq (the majority of the film) with his life back home, where he has a wife and an infant son. By observing his inability to relate to life in the United States, James's actual attachment to his job in Iraq comes into focus. Prior to the scene in the cereal aisle, viewers encounter him cleaning his house's gutters with a discontented expression. We could say, as we did in discussing other characters above, that "home" is no longer home to James. That is, it is no longer a place of familiarity and comfort. Like Yates, James finds that everything has changed, perhaps because he has changed. He offers a monologue to his baby at the end of the film that provides a sentiment similar to the one expressed by Yates:

> You love playing with all your stuffed animals. You love your Mommy, your Daddy. You love your pajamas. You love everything, don't ya? Yea[h]. But you know what, buddy? As you get older . . . some of the things you love might not seem so special anymore. Like your jack-in-a-box. Maybe you'll realize it's just a piece of tin and a stuffed animal. And the older you get, the fewer things you really love. And by the time you get to my age, maybe it's only one or two things. With me, I think it's one.

With this, James returns to diffusing bombs in Iraq—the one thing that viewers can infer he really loves. It is through a commitment to redeployment that, from the perspective of Hollywood, the wars being fought by James and Yates must be engaged. It is no accident that both of these soldiers are white and male, given the role of white maleness in shouldering what has obviously become the 9/11 burden. According to official and presidential rhetoric, the United States is fighting the War on Terror on foreign soil as a response to a war that began at home. The message is that 9/11 is in these soldiers, as it is "in" New York, the Pentagon, Pennsylvania, and America more broadly. Places once considered safe are no longer safe. In the face of displacement, Americans do "what needs to be done"—fight, and presumably win, the war(s) thrust upon them. In the end, reenlistment is primarily the responsibility of white men, since the burden of 9/11 falls squarely on their shoulders. However, whether redeployment alleviates internal conflict and renders a resolution to (American) displacement after September 11, 2001, remains unresolved in these films. In addition, the fact that the soldiers in both films returned from Iraq, the lesser-supported war engagement, might make it easier for producers and directors to convey their message about these soldiers and the War on Terror, as well as what viewers are supposed to feel toward them and it.

V FOR VENDETTA AND *AVATAR*: CONTAINMENT OF SEXUALIZED/RACIALIZED THREATS

According to Andrew Schopp, along with other films, *V for Vendetta* (2006) "depict[s] the way governments, media, and/or individuals manipulate fear . . . [speaking] to the contemporary cultural and political condition in America, a situation in which fear threatens to function as a means of social and political control" (2009, 260). In fact, when discussing *V for Vendetta*, critics have tended to focus on similarities between the fictitious fascist regime of Chancellor Adam Sutler (John Hurt) and the actual presidency of George W. Bush. Even Alan Moore, creator of the original *V for Vendetta* graphic novel, criticized Hollywood's version of his art for its desire to transform it into a critique of President Bush and his administration (*Infoshop.org* 2010).

While it perhaps hides behind a futuristic scenario unfolding in Britain, *V for Vendetta* nonetheless offers similarities between the discourses of Chancellor Sutler and President Bush in a 9/11 United States. Below is just one example of this similarity. Here, Chancellor Sutler warns of an impending attack from V:

> Tonight our country, that which we stand for, and all we hold dear, faces a grave and terrible threat. This violent and unparalleled assault on our security will not go undefended. Our enemy is an insidious one, seeking to divide us and destroy the very foundation of our great nation. Tonight, we must remain steadfast. We must remain determined. But most of all, we must remain united.

Below, President Bush conveys the lesson of 9/11:

> Great harm has been done to us. We have suffered great loss. And in our grief and anger we have found our mission and our moment. Freedom and fear are at war. The advance of human freedom—the great achievement of our time, and the great hope of every time—now depends on us. . . . We will rally the world to this cause by our efforts, by our courage. We will not tire, we will not falter, and we will not fail. (2001a)

Although political rhetoric is central to our argument regarding the construction of 9/11 and the *9/11 project*, rather than highlight further dramatized similarities between Chancellor Sutler's regime and the G. W. Bush administration, we would like to focus on the film's lessons surrounding sexuality and race/ethnicity, including militarized responses to them. This particular aspect of the film presents the most extreme manifestation of the us/them rhetoric emerging after September 11, 2001, and provides an excellent example of conflations of otherwise distinct issues. As we argue elsewhere, "Throughout the G. W. Bush [9/11] era, various bodies and issues were systematically intertwined and conflated" (Bloodsworth-Lugo and Lugo-Lugo 2010, 1). For instance, the president routinely discussed Iraq, the War on Terror, the economy, immigration, and his views on same-sex marriage in the same addresses and news conferences in which he articulated general threats to Americans. This move was so consistent and successful that these topics came to link "in the minds of the American public" and the associated bodies (terrorists, immigrants, gays) "were rendered in need of strict containment" (Bloodsworth-Lugo and Lugo-Lugo 2010, 1).

In *V for Vendetta*, viewers witness a conflation between V, as a terrorist threat, and the threat of homosexuality. The film uses the character of Valerie (Natasha Wightman)—whom viewers later learn has been long dead—to narrate a story within the plot. The story reveals a perfect analogy between the treatment of sexuality (gay men and lesbians, in particular) under Sutler's regime and past historical occurrences involving race and ethnicity; most notably, the Jewish Holocaust under Nazi Germany, the massive deportation of Mexicans that occurred in the United States in the 1930s, and the treatment of American Indians within the history of the United States. It is also a reminder of ballot initiatives within the United States after September 11, 2001, advancing constitutional amendments to ban same-sex marriage, especially from 2003 onward. These initiatives were a highly supported project by President Bush, and voters responded by linking disparate issues at the ballot box as part of the ideology of the *9/11 project*. As discussed in chapter 1, an important component of the ideologies embedded within the *9/11 project* in the United States has been transforming particular bodies and markers into perceived threats. From efforts to thwart state sanctions of same-sex relationships, to backlash over the ordination of the first gay bishop by the Episcopal Church USA, to the prisoner abuse scandal at Abu Ghraib prison, objection to nonstraight sexualities has figured prominently in 9/11 American discourse and culture. Within the United States, the containment of sexuality and the bodies of those deemed deviant intensified during the first decade of the twenty-first century in tandem with political and militarized efforts to contain terrorists, immigrants, and other groups considered outside the fold of the U.S. mainstream (Bloodsworth-Lugo and Lugo-Lugo 2010).

Interestingly, *V for Vendetta* is not a story about sexuality, at least not straightforwardly, as the film tells the story of Evey (Natalie Portman), a young girl in Sutler's regime, who is rescued from the police by V (Hugo Weaving). As the story unfolds, Evey, whose parents died fighting Sutler's regime when she was a child, is forced by V to learn about history in a rather brutal way: He holds her prisoner and treats her the way prisoners are treated under the regime. During this time, Evey learns about Valerie, and ultimately, Evey ends up sympathizing with V and his cause. The film places emphasis on the role of memory ("remember, remember the 5th of November"), as most of what Evey learns is through the past and through Valerie's story. Valerie, viewers come to learn, is no longer alive, and it is through her story as a lesbian that Evey discovers the treatment of nondominant sexualities under Sutler's rule. However, before viewers actually learn about the treatment of gay men and lesbians through the film, two important points surface: There is a strong and consistent use of the term "we" when articulating how circumstances are and ought to be by the government and the media, and gay men and lesbians are shown to be incapable of living their lives openly within the film's setting.

Viewers first encounter the second issue when Evey's coworker, Gordon Dietrich (Stephen Fry), "comes out" to her. As Gordon tells Evey, "You wear a mask for so long, you forget who you were beneath it." Viewers learn that Gordon must not only hide his sexuality but also any material indication that he may not be straight, such as his interest in literature, music, and art. Thus, when viewers begin to learn Valerie's story, they are already positioned to know that it will not end well. Valerie provides her account through Evey, who reads installments of the story while imprisoned by V. The narration begins as follows, "I remember how the meaning of words began to change. How unfamiliar words like 'collateral' and 'rendition' became frightening. I remember how 'different' became dangerous. I still don't understand it, why they hate us so much." The words "collateral" and "rendition," along with the phrase "why they hate us so much," serve as anchors and references for Americans watching the film, for they are parts of the lexicon of the *9/11 project*. The story continues and culminates when Valerie finds Ruth (Mary Stockley), the love of her life. After conveying how happy they were together, Evey describes, in Valerie's words, an event closely reminiscent of the historical and more recent events referenced above: "They took Ruth while she was out buying food. I've never cried so hard in my life. It wasn't long till they came for me."

We agree with Alan Moore's critique of Hollywood's treatment of *V for Vendetta*'s material. While the setting of the film is Britain, the allegories, along with Natalie Portman's presence (as Evey), offer a decidedly American point of view—and a 9/11 view, in particular. Consequently, American viewers of the film are able to accommodate the film's messages within their frames of vision and modes of understanding in a 9/11 United States. Moreover, in a film almost completely devoid of racial content, an embattled Valerie, wondering why she (as a lesbian) is so hated, harkens to the experiences of racial minorities who have asked similar questions for most of the existence of the United States. In this case, the treatment of sexuality is used as a substitute for race, offering a futuristic concentration camp, or Abu Ghraib-like prison, while conjuring the conceived threat of sexual outsiders in a 9/11 America. It also provides a warning of what could happen—both to the subjects themselves and to the contours of the country if permitted to continue down a similar path. This is why the statement, "It wasn't long until they came for me," is so haunting.

The film *Avatar* (2009) has been heralded as a welcome critique of environmental destruction and pervasive military actions. Writing for CNN.com, movie critic Tom Charity remarks that *Avatar* "wears its anti-imperialist, anti-corporate sentiments on its sleeve" (2009). However, Charity also indicates that this message is rather ironic given the status of the film as a "big, big budget blockbuster, a movie that seems destined to inflate Hollywood costs still further at a time when mid-budget pictures are being squeezed out" (2009). In addition to its denunciation of imperialism and rampant corporatization, viewers can find in *Avatar* a message regarding 9/11 and the *9/11 project*—even when its setting is another planet (or moon) in the twenty-second century.

The film relays the story of the Na'vi, the native inhabitants of Pandora, a moon replete with "Unobtanium"—a precious metal desired and needed by Americans to solve their energy crisis. The Na'vi, along with their Tree of Life, sit atop the richest deposit of the mineral known to humans. In the words of Parker Selfridge (Giovanni Ribisi), a representative of the corporation aiming to sell the mineral in the film, "This is why we are here [showing a small rock]: Because this little grey rock sells for 20 million a kilo. Their village happens to be resting on the richest deposit and they need to relocate. Those savages are threatening our whole operation." The extraction has become a corporate and military operation, as scientists working for both the U.S. military and the company in charge of mining Unobtanium have developed specific avatars to gain access to the planet, which is toxic to humans, and its people, who are much taller and stronger. Viewers learn that Marine Jake Sully (Sam Worthington) has been brought to Pandora to replace his twin brother, Tom, a scientist who has died. Since Jake and Tom are identical twins, Jake provides a genetic match for Tom's avatar.

Although the plot is reminiscent of many imperialist efforts within human history, the dialogue reveals a uniqueness vis-à-vis 9/11. For instance, in one of his video journals, Jake confides, "This is how it's done. When people are sitting on shit that you want, you make 'em your enemy. Then you're justified in taking it." Jake is saying this while dressing in his military uniform, which might help American viewers consider him in the same light as soldiers in Afghanistan or Iraq filming similar video diaries. In addition, Jake's candid interpretation of the situation in Pandora is quite similar to critics' claims of the United States' occupation of Iraq as being tied to oil and, similarly, of President Bush's transformation of former President Saddam Hussein into an enemy to enable the invasion of Iraq, which would allow access to that oil.

The film's dialogue also utilizes the "us/them" rhetoric consistently employed by President Bush and the Bush administration to reference terrorists. When Colonel Quaritch (Stephen Lang), Jake's commanding officer, learns that Jake is more sympathetic to the Na'vi than the military operation demands, he remarks, "You let me down, son! So, you find yourself some local tail, and you just completely forget what team you're playin' for? Hey Sully . . . how does it feel to betray your own race? You think you're one of them?" The mark of 9/11 is also clearly seen in Colonel Quaritch's rant when preparing the troops for combat against the Na'vi, in which he says, "We can't wait. Our only security lies in preemptive attack. We will fight terror with terror. When we destroy [this mountain stronghold], we will blast a crater in their racial memory so deep, they won't come within a thousand licks of this place." The call for preemptive attack, fighting terror with terror, and blasting the hostiles back in time recall the "Shock and Awe" campaign in Iraq and comprise central components of the collective discourse deployed to address "terrorists" after September 11, 2001.

Thus, it is no coincidence that when Jake Sully (or his avatar) falls in love with Neytiri (Zoe Saldaña), a female Na'vi, the lure of the female native (the "hostile") becomes a threat to the United States and its corporate and military interests. Colonel Quaritch's reproach of Jake—that he has betrayed his own "race" for a piece of "local tail"—is telling in this regard. Even if we were to assume that the colonel intends to reference the human race in general, and not a particular race within the broader category, the situation would present itself as still more complicated, given that the entire film revolves around U.S. military and corporate interests. So, when Quaritch refers to "race," he may actually mean to suggest that the United States is a race, and although viewers might assume that the Earth's energy crisis is a global situation, the scientists, the corporate representatives, the military personnel, and the avatars in the film are exclusively American. Moreover, the colonel, the lead scientist and her assistant, the lead corporate representative, and Jake are all *white* Americans. The use of the word "race" by Quaritch could very well suggest that Americans are being equated with the human race and that the human race is incompatible with the Na'vi. The Bush administration consistently deployed a similar equation, suggesting that some bodies undermine the whole of human/Western civilization and threaten the recognized pillars of humanity themselves.

CONCLUSION

While sexuality and race have not been the primary areas of concern for most commentators and critics of *V for Vendetta* and *Avatar*, these issues nonetheless place both films squarely within the ideological space of the *9/11 project*. Although we can identify other moments in U.S. history in which sexuality has been racialized and race has been sexualized, this comingling of issues has been persistent within the 9/11 era and a staple of the official discourse of the G. W. Bush administration. Consider, for instance, the juxtaposition of the following statements—one in opposition to same-sex marriage and the other concerning national security: "Our nation must defend the sanctity of marriage"; "America will never seek a permission slip to defend the security of our country" (Bush 2004). The president continues, "Inside the United States, where the war began, we must continue to give homeland security and law enforcement personnel every tool they need to defend us" (Bush 2004). All statements are from President Bush's 2004 State of the Union address, and the deployment of the phrase "to defend" is consistent in all three—regardless of the fact that within a different context, "the sanctity of marriage" would have nothing to do with national security.

As a result, Americans and American popular culture were subjected to seven years of persistent conflations and discourse involving sexualized and racialized threats to the nation. These threats became part of Americans' ideological framework and components of the *9/11 project*, as illustrated within the films discussed above. Gay men and lesbians have been conflated with terrorist threats, terrorists have been identified and reified as another race, gay men and lesbians have been racialized, and racialized threats have become sites of requisite containment (Bloodsworth-Lugo and Lugo-Lugo 2010). The American public ("us") has been separated from terrorists ("them"), while the range and realm of perceived terrorist threats have expanded. Importantly, these conflations of threat, a central component of the *9/11 project*, are recreated and portrayed in Hollywood mainstream films after September 11, 2001, even when those films do not mention 9/11 or the events of September 11, 2001.

Interestingly, even within such films with fantastical settings, white American men (or their avatars) assume the burden of 9/11. This burden is perhaps depicted more realistically or directly in films featuring soldiers and war, such as *Home of the Brave* and

The Hurt Locker, in which soldiers respond to threat, insecurity, and loss of familiarity/home, by returning to sites of war. This "going back" reflects a way of shouldering (white, American, male) burdens in the wake of 9/11. While the ideological reverberations of 9/11 take multiple shapes, these shapes link to form a singular story—one of threats and fears, annihilation and containment, all within an unprecedented landscape. In 9/11 films, the concept of 9/11 has unfolded to represent an emerging U.S. society after "the day that changed America and the world forever."

Pollard suggests that the 9/11 era may become known as "the age of paranoia" (2009, 206). And Schopp contends that viewing some films released after September 11, 2001, reveals that 9/11 American culture is one "troubled by its media, torn between conflicted visions of justice, bogged down in moral complexity yet desiring no moral ambiguity and thus unable to determine where 'evil' and 'good' truly reside" (2009, 281). In the second edition to his now-classic book *Movie-Made America*, published seven years prior to September 11, 2001, Robert Sklar argues that by the early 1990s, no social commentator "could speak confidently of the magic and myth of the movies" after "decades of turmoil and transformation—within the film industry and in society at large—had taken their toll on Hollywood's capacity to purvey America's myths and dreams" (1994, 357). He blames multiculturalism for this loss by reasoning, "The cultural disunity of American society gave rise to a new concern, not with the traditional rhetoric of myths and dreams, but with historical memory" (358). For Sklar, multiculturalism has created a sort of fractured society preoccupied with its past instead of its future.

While we disagree with Sklar's claim regarding multiculturalism and its effect on society and film, we can clearly see that the *9/11 project* has changed film in a fundamental way in which neither historical memory nor myths or dreams are a primary concern. The concept of 9/11 has provided a lens for the American public through which to interpret their present—a present completely devoid of a past and one that anticipates an uncertain, but yet threatening, future. In the process, it has also unified an American public intent on containing threats and fears. This intent is reflected in 9/11 films, given that these films likewise reveal a consistent effort to contain new threats, amorphous threats, threats that will continue, and threats that came to our shores on one fateful day that shaped the contours of our perception of reality, perhaps forever.

Chapter Four

Narratives of Threat and 9/11 Monsters

Tales of a battle between good and evil must depict the world as a threatening or even terrifying place, full of monsters. That alone would be enough to make people feel insecure. But there is more. The stories always imply (and often say quite openly) that the monsters can never be destroyed. The best to hope for is to build a stout defense against them, one strong enough to keep them from destroying us. The monsters may be contained. But their threat will never go away. (Chernus 2006, 4–5)

In April 2013, a *Washington Post* poll asked Americans whether they worried more about the U.S. government not going far enough in investigating "terrorism because of concerns about constitutional rights," or whether they worried more about the government going "too far in compromising constitutional rights in order to investigate terrorism" (WP Politics 2013). The results showed that, with a 48 percent to 41 percent split, Americans worried more that the government would go too far in investigating terrorism than that the government would not do enough to investigate terrorism (WP Politics 2013). The results of the poll show a certain amount of weariness by Americans concerning the reach of government after September 11, 2001. This notion contrasts markedly with responses to another question showing that 66 percent of Americans thought "the terrorists will always find a way to launch major attacks no matter what the government does." The question, then, would be, if Americans think that the government is becoming too forceful, and regardless of governmental actions terrorists will continue to wreak havoc, what options are available to citizens? In an October 2013 ABC News interview, Interpol Secretary General Ronald Noble (an American) offers two options for preventing situations in which crowds of civilians or "soft targets" are attacked by terrorists: "Either create secure perimeters around the locations or allow civilians to carry their own guns to protect themselves" (Margolin 2013).

The films in this chapter explore notions surrounding an ineffective or deceitful U.S. infrastructure, represented by the government or more specifically governmental workers, and ways in which citizens are forced by circumstances to "take matters into their own hands." In all three films addressed below, *Flightplan* (2005), *Lakeview Terrace* (2008), and *The Brave One* (2007), evil is depicted via isolated acts of terrorism in the form of attacks against the films' main characters. Taking charge of these situations recalls tropes associated with the vulnerability, insecurity, and burden of white American men, discussed in previous chapters. And the events unfolding in these films speak to the idea of a changed America, in which threats lurk in shadows or are assumed to reside everywhere. The films in this chapter can be distinguished from those previously analyzed, however, in two fundamental ways: Citizens take charge of events with no direct or indirect connection to September 11, 2001, or its wars, and white women are introduced as sometimes sharing the insecurity and burden of 9/11 with white men—albeit with certain gendered differences that we will discuss.

9/11 CITIZENS AND 9/11 MONSTERS

In the chapter's opening epigraph, Chernus speaks to both historical and contemporary, or 9/11, articulations of the quintessential conflict between good and evil as they are embedded within U.S. ideologies. Within the 9/11 era, the American battle with evil entails a conflict with an un-American enemy or terrorist body. We can locate formulations and ideological articulations of the constant—but ever-changing—battle described by Chernus within the rhetorical techniques deployed by former president Bush during his time in office, encompassing the seven years after September 11, 2001. Rhetorical strategies of the Bush administration are of central importance to our analysis in this project, since their immediate articulation and consistent deployment as a response to the events of September 11, 2001, helped to shape the 9/11 American lens. In fact, this lens still informs much of the American landscape and provides an enduring feature of our national discourse, even in the wake of the country's election of its first black president, Barack Obama, and a change of national leadership in 2008–2009 (see Bloodsworth-Lugo and Lugo-Lugo 2010).

As we argue elsewhere, the repetition of us versus them discourse not only merged otherwise separate and distinct issues, it reinforced a series of oppositional pairings, such as inside/outside and safety/threat, enabling the American public to conceive of the United States as a vulnerable place in light of the September 11, 2001, events. The discourse likewise constructed the American people, the country, and even (Western) civilization itself as requiring vigilant protection (Bloodsworth-Lugo and Lugo-Lugo 2010). Security and protection thereby became synonymous with the containment of threats, and as discussed previously, these notions have become lasting staples of the ideology comprising the *9/11 project*.

After several years of diligent enemy construction during his administration, President Bush warned in his 2007 State of the Union address, "By killing and terrorizing Americans, [our enemies] want to force our country to retreat from the world and abandon the cause of liberty. They would then be free to impose their will and spread their totalitarian ideology" (Bush 2007). The president added, "It remains the policy of this government to use every lawful and proper tool of intelligence, diplomacy, law enforcement, and military action to do our duty, to find these enemies, and to protect the American people" (Bush 2007). Keeping with Chernus, we could say that the construction of these very threats captured and promoted a particular conception and perception of 9/11 enemies and monsters for the American public.

Throughout his time in office, President Bush's speeches convey the enemy as a cruel opponent of freedom—placing no value on life and aiming to impose an empire of oppression with brutal rulers to terrorize and kill Americans. According to Richard Jackson, "the [Bush] administration was quick to identify the terrorists as 'evil,' 'savage,' 'cruel,' 'cowardly,' 'inhuman,' 'hate-filled,' 'perverted,' and 'alien'" (2009, 27). Jackson identifies two central features of this narrative pertinent to the present chapter: first, the suggestion of "a massive, global terrorist threat against Americans and their way of life," as well as civilization more broadly construed (which we address more fully in chapter 5); and second, the invocation of the "notion of 'the enemy within,'" implying that the American public "should remain watchful of fellow citizens, and that measures designed to restrict liberties, increase surveillance on U.S. citizens and immigrants, and further militarize American society were necessary to counter the threat of these internal enemies" (2009, 27). We will return to Jackson's notion of "the enemy within" shortly, as it specifically informs our analysis of films in this chapter.

As discussed throughout this book, 9/11 films have developed their narratives and tropes within this context. Many of the stories within these films reflect American fears and anxieties, even if the films themselves do not directly address the events of September 11, 2001, as we demonstrated in the previous chapter and continue here. In chapter 1, we cited Pollard, who argues that filmmakers responded to the events of September 11, 2001, "by producing some of the most pessimistic, violent, cynical movies of all time," while simultaneously projecting "powerful fantasy heroes capable of redressing all wrongs" (2009, 206). This state of affairs leads Pollard to conclude, "Apparently, widespread fear engenders strong characters, pessimistic moods, critical examinations of intelligence agencies, and a cynical perspective on a variety of social institutions including U.S. corporations, military, and government" (206). In our analyses below, we focus on the blending of strong characters, pessimistic moods, and cynical portrayals of state institutions provided by Hollywood mainstream films. We also follow Markovitz's position that although the entity known as Hollywood "has a long history of turning widespread fears into cinematic spectacles, never before has the source of those fears been so singular, so easily isolated, or so thoroughly disseminated to national and international audiences" (2004, 201). Fear is a motivating element of the *9/11 project*, and while not a particularly straightforward phenomenon to document, Hollywood films do offer an important venue for recording and analyzing social fears.

Kyle Bishop sheds light on this topic by conveying:

> The terrorist attacks of September 11, 2001, caused perhaps the largest wave of paranoia for Americans since the McCarthy era. Since the beginning of the war on terror, American popular culture has been colored by the fear of possible terrorist attacks and the grim realization that people are not as safe and secure as they might have once thought. (2009, 17)

These and other critical media scholars highlight the fact that 9/11 films develop a particular discourse and ideology (one that we link to the fears and anxieties embedded within the *9/11 project*), while simultaneously leveling critiques of that project, and doing so without specific reference to the events of September 11, 2001. In general, then, 9/11 films examine American anxieties in the wake of a changed America, including how Americans might respond to and ultimately cope with an increasing number of 9/11 monsters, while simultaneously relegating September 11, 2001, itself to an unspoken background. Antonio Sanchez-Escalonilla notes that in the fictional works of Hollywood, "Though direct references to the tragic day are avoided, there is a hypothetical discourse of contribution to the political debate, and often solutions are suggested to alleviate the social fractures, but always in the guise of entertainment" (2010, 11). Jackson adds to this point, "[Actions and events] take on different kinds and levels of meaning for a political community through processes of interpretation and social narration, usually by the powerful symbolic actors authorized to speak on behalf of the whole community" (2009, 25).

Below, we explore connections between 9/11 articulations of the enemy as threat and representations in recent Hollywood films. We agree with Bishop, when commenting on zombie films after September 11, 2001, that while central "plot elements and motifs are present in zombie films before September 11, 2001, they have become more relevant to a modern, contemporary audience" (2009, 20). We maintain that while genre protocols may offer consistency before and after September 11, 2001, ways of managing fears and anxieties around threats and vigilance assume a particular relevance to 9/11 American viewers. Each film discussed below presents a specific threat, as well as an enacted response, underscoring themes of terror and vigilance in a 9/11 world.

Finally, before analysis of the films as such, we would like to clarify our use of the monster. In a sense, the films below offer us a straightforward *monsterification* of certain people and places in a decidedly 9/11 way—that is, by presenting amorphous terroristic threats in the shapely form of a monster. However, the monster does not have a consistent representation, for at times it is portrayed as an external/outside nearby threat; other times, it is portrayed as residing within—within our borders, communities, and selves. Thus, representations of the monster in these films are a synthesis of both outside and inside threats. Keeping with Jackson, we link an examination of the enemy within to 9/11 threats in two particular ways: the enemy/monster as *place* and the enemy/monster as *person*. We note a movement, or a transformation, from familiar terrain (such as knowledge of oneself, expectations around the role of authority figures, or the look and feel of one's city or neighborhood) to unfamiliar territory (such as becoming a stranger to oneself, being threatened by those with authority, or facing insecurity within one's typical place of comfort). Moreover, we observe a betrayal of borders and boundaries—an invasion of the familiar—within these and similar films. This betrayal demonstrates new anxieties, or a new inflection to continuing fears and anxieties, within a 9/11 United States. As Marina Levina and Diem-My Bui convey, "While monsters [have] always tapped into anxieties over a changing world, they have never been as popular or as needed as in the last decade" (2013, 2).

FLIGHTPLAN : THE ENEMY/MONSTER ON BOARD

Flightplan develops the uncertainty of threats lurking in shadows and lingering among us in relation to an American mother, Kyle Pratt (Jodie Foster), who is attempting to protect and recover her six-year-old daughter, Julia (Marlene Lawston), from an amorphous threat on board an airplane. Pratt, a propulsion engineer, is returning her dead husband's body to the United States from Germany when she loses her daughter on an air jet—the "biggest plane of them all." Mirroring a 9/11 rhetoric of threats, *Flightplan* presents a danger that is difficult to identify insofar as its source is unclear. Pratt spends the majority of the film attempting to determine the exact nature and cause of the threat, knowing only that her child is missing when she (Pratt) awakens from a nap.

The fact that Pratt is highly knowledgeable regarding the air jet's structure and equipment casts her uncertainty about the daughter's whereabouts on the plane as all the more terrifying for view-

ers, since even within Pratt's familiar environment lurks an unde-
tected and ominous danger. To place the air jet in the role of a 9/11
United States, the plot suggests that citizens and even leaders of a
country might be unable to account for threats lurking in the recess-
es of its borders, since monsters often have incomprehensible de-
signs and sinister intentions. Pratt, and the film in general, attends
to the perceived threat of any and all Muslims/Arabs as obvious 9/
11 sites of enemy/monster construction. As Manohla Dargis conveys, the film contains "some shameless nods to September 11"
(2005). These nods are displayed when Pratt targets the airplane's
male Middle Eastern passengers for her daughter's disappearance.
Pratt states to the air marshal, Gene Carson (Peter Sarsgaard), after
confronting one of these men, "I don't give a shit about being
politically correct! I think they're hijacking the plane. I think my
daughter's a hostage."

While anxiously searching for her daughter, Pratt herself is
turned into a safety threat given rules concerning airline passenger
conduct after September 11, 2001. Carson is first to position Pratt
this way when she attempts to barge into the cockpit after realizing
her daughter is not in the passenger areas of the plane. Carson
restrains Pratt and tells her, "I'm sorry I had to do that, but your
behavior was constituting a threat to the safety of this aircraft."
Pratt then asks to enter the plane's cargo hold—again, knowing the
plane's layout quite well and not seeing her daughter in the passenger areas. Carson offers to accompany her, but Captain Rich (Sean
Bean) dismisses this suggestion, stating, "Mister Carson, I'm responsible for the safety of every passenger on this plane, even the
delusional ones." When Pratt voices her impatience with the captain and crew, Captain Rich remarks, "There are 425 passengers on
this flight who are NOT receiving any attention at the moment
because every one of my flight attendants are [sic] looking for a
child that none of them believe was ever on board."

Pratt is declared mentally unstable after the crew searches for the girl within the plane's infrastructure, yielding no results. The captain is handed an official document stating that the child was killed, along with Pratt's husband, when they both fell from the rooftop of their house in Germany. The paperwork, combined with the fact that Julia is not listed on the passenger manifest and no one remembers seeing her board the plane, convinces the captain and crew that the child was actually never present. Instead, they infer that Pratt is suffering from extreme anxiety and grief, rendering her delusional. In turn, it is this delusion and its attendant behavior that constitute a threat. As Carson explains, "I'm responsible for anything that might become a threat to the safety of this flight. Women with imaginary children qualify."

Near the end of the film, viewers learn that the air marshal himself (along with a crew member accomplice) kidnapped Pratt's daughter, hid her within the cargo hold of the plane, fabricated the paperwork deleting the child from the passenger manifest, documenting that she had died, and smuggled in explosives. Once Pratt realizes that Carson is the cause of her daughter's disappearance, she takes matters into her own hands. Pratt locates the child and explosives in avionics (where she always thought the child was being hidden). After the plane has landed and she, her daughter, and the other passengers are secure, Pratt allows the explosives to detonate with Carson still inside the plane. We see Pratt transformed, during this one flight and its attendant ordeal, from an anxious and grieving widow/mother into a person capable of destroying a plane with someone else on board. Prior to her exit, Carson asks, "What are you gonna do? Blow us both up?" Pratt coolly and calmly responds, "No, just you."

This film conveys to 9/11 viewers that familiar spaces can quickly and radically transform into unfamiliar sites. With this transformation, one's sense of familiarity gives way to unfamiliarity—evoking a monstrous response. Carson is easily identifiable as the film's bad guy (at least, by the end of the film), and his badness is made all the more salient given his role to protect the plane's passengers. This sort of danger lingering among us is one way in which 9/11 narrative has unfolded. However, it is Pratt's own transformation—from loving and grieving mother to person capable of destroying what she had designed (the plane) with Carson on board—that demonstrates an even more disturbing example of the enemy/monster within. Unlike Carson, who is killed at the end of the film (Pratt's enacted solution to his threat), Pratt's own transformation remains unresolved with the film's end.

LAKEVIEW TERRACE:
THE ENEMY/MONSTER NEXT DOOR

Similar to *Flightplan*, *Lakeview Terrace* develops the notion of threats lurking in shadows and lingering among us primarily in relation to two characters. These characters are a police officer, Abel Turner (Samuel L. Jackson), and a supermarket chain executive, Chris Mattson (Patrick Wilson). With the tagline "What could be safer than living next to a cop?" the film is set in a suburban neighborhood in Southern California, and the plot is replete with racial and racist innuendo involving Turner who is black, Mattson who is white, and Mattson's wife, Lisa (Kerry Washington), who is black. Unlike Carson in *Flightplan*, who is only unveiled as a threat at the end of the film, the threat that Turner poses, especially to Chris and Lisa—who have just moved in next door—is demonstrated early. *Flightplan* and *Lakeview Terrace* are similar in that the people assigned to be protector (air marshal and police officer) instead transform into the enemies the main characters are required to guard against.

Viewers receive a clear indication of Turner's views on racial mixing, which is the locus of his threat to the mixed-race couple, in an opening scene of the film. Here, Turner is detaining Clarence

Darlington (Keith Loneker), an overweight white-looking infor-
mant, when Darlington refers to Turner as "brother." The following
exchange ensues:

> Turner: Brother? Clarence, we ain't brothers. We didn't even
> crawl out of the same evolutionary pool. What are you, anyway?
> You know, always wondered about that. You a Euro-Mexi-Japa-
> Chine-stani or what? You don't even know, do you? Ain't got a
> clue.

> Informant: Watch yourself.

> Turner: You're a weed, that's what you are. A junkyard weed.
> Spray your ass with some Roundup.

> Informant: I'm 1/7th Cherokee, bitch!

> Turner: Yeah, and the other 93 percent wigger. Can you do the
> math on that, dumb ass?

On Turner's first encounter with Mattson, it is Mattson's taste in
music that grounds Turner's negative racial commentary. Viewers
see that, as Mattson returns home from work, he is playing loud
hip-hop music in his car. After walking over to the car, introducing
himself, and making a few crude remarks, Turner finally tells Mattson, "Say, you know, you can listen to that noise all night long, but
when you wake up in the morning, you'll still be white." And
somewhat later in the film, while giving Mattson a tour of the
neighborhood, Turner bluntly says, "You know, I got nothing
against you. Or her. LAPD. I work with all kinds. I'd lay my life
down for those guys. But that's where I work. This is where I live."
Turner's desire for the couple to leave *his* neighborhood is expressed on multiple occasions and in ever more threatening ways as
the film progresses. The film highlights the escalating conflict between Turner and Mattson, as Mattson attempts to claim his role as

protector of his family (Lisa is pregnant) and to reposition his authority as a white man within society. While the notion of a black
man posing a threat to a white person is not new (for example,
historical notions of black men as brutes or savages), what is new
in *Lakeview Terrace* is the 9/11 construction of this particular
threat. Turner resides within the fold of the law, as cop, but he uses
that location and role to wield his own agenda—and that agenda
plays out in the nice suburban neighborhood in which he and the
couple live. As a black cop making a threat against a mixed-race
couple, and primarily the white character, Mattson, the film's presentation of threat suggests an uncertainty given a sort of familiarity.
That is, the threat resides in relation to a presumed protector and
within one's own neighborhood. Additionally, the film implies that
white Americans are on their own, in charge of protecting themselves and their families from the danger "lurking in the shadows of
suburbia" (Scott 2008). Here, suburbia is transformed from a familiar and safe place (for white folks, especially) into one that is housing enemies/monsters—ones lingering as close as next door.

Interestingly, the film also inverts history, since the threat that
blacks have faced in the hands of whites dates to colonial times.
This suggests that in an America scarred by the events of September 11, 2001, white Americans in particular have experienced an
unsettling territory in new ways. Like Kyle Pratt (discussed above)
and Erica Bain (discussed below), Chris Mattson is himself transformed into something monstrous through his solution to the unfolding problem. This is another case in which the vulnerability and
insecurity experienced by whites turns into a burden, for at these
moments, when these characters take action, they transform into
something else. In this particular film, while Mattson does not
shoot and kill Abel Turner within the film, he is nonetheless quite
ready to do so. Instead, Mattson allows Turner's colleagues to take
the shot for him, resulting in Turner's death near the film's end.
Mattson and his wife must find a way to move forward after this

resolution, leaving the ways in which Mattson has been transformed unresolved, much like the transformation of Pratt in *Flightplan*.

THE BRAVE ONE: THE STRANGER/MONSTER INSIDE

In *The Brave One*, the main character, Erica Bain (Jodie Foster), describes New York as "an organism that changes, mutates." In a narration opening the film, she conveys:

> I'm Erica Bain. And as you know, I walk the city. I bitch and moan about it. I walk and watch and listen, a witness to all the beauty and ugliness that is disappearing from our beloved city. Last week took me to the gray depths of the East River where Dmitri Panchenko swims his morning laps, like he has every morning since the 1960s. And today I walked by the acres of scaffolding outside what used to be the Plaza Hotel. And I thought about Eloise. Remember Kay Thompson's Eloise? Stories of a city that is disappearing before our eyes. So what are we left of those stories? Are we going to have to construct an imaginary city to house our memories? Because when you love something, every time a bit goes, you lose a piece of yourself.

At the end of the narration, we learn that Bain has a radio show: "This is Erica Bain, and you've been listening to *Streetwalk* on WKNW."

Bain's fiancé is beaten to death during a nighttime stroll with their dog, as the couple discuss their plans for marriage. Like the September 11, 2001, attacks on the city, the attack on the couple arrives out of the blue, on a beautiful and otherwise normal day, with the sound of a passing airplane foreshadowing the horror of the event. With this event, Bain devolves into a vigilante killer—someone "fearing the place [she] once loved" and acting to protect the city and herself. She finds herself transformed into a stranger that both enacts justice for the death of her fiancé (killing eight men, including the three men who attacked her and her fiancé) and develops a close friendship with a detective, Mercer (Terrence Howard), investigating the deaths. Bain discovers in herself a monstrous inside to match a monstrous outside. She also faces an uncertain future involving an expanding array of "monsters to destroy." However, she finds in herself a power she did not know existed.

Discussing the film, Claire S. King compares the trauma experienced by Bain to an allegory of sorts, invoking, constructing, and making sense "of national history and identity, framing 9/11 as a culturally traumatic event" (2010, 111). King continues:

> Bain's assertions of mastery perform a fantasy of national resilience, and her transformation enacts the nation's attempts to convert itself from a feminized victim to a (re)masculinized agent. With her search for victims and stalking of predators recalling President Bush's commitment "to hunt down, to find, to smoke out of their holes" the terrorists he held responsible for 9/11, Bain's ability to remain "brave" rewrites the nation's response to perceived trauma and redresses what has been framed as weakness, or paternal failure, on the part of America. (2010, 123)

The traumatic event that Bain endures can be described as "the day that changed Erica forever," while Bain's response to that event works to transform her into a stranger to herself. For our purposes, it is Bain's understanding of and struggle with her own transformation that is most significant. Viewers receive glimpses into her struggle throughout the film. For instance, Bain states, "It is astonishing, numbing to find that inside you there is a stranger. One that has your arms, your legs, your eyes. A sleepless, restless stranger who keeps walking, keeps eating, keeps living." Upon returning to work, she conveys to her radio listeners:

> I always believed that fear belonged to other people. Weaker people. It never touched me. And then it did. And when it touches you, you know that it's been there all along. Waiting

beneath the surfaces of everything you loved. And your skin crawls, and your heart sickens, and you look at the person you once were walking down that street and you wonder will you . . . will you ever be her again?

Importantly, Bain conceptualizes the stranger as a thing. After killing her fourth victim, she remarks, "There is no going back to that other. She is gone. This thing, this stranger is all you are now." Here, the stranger is exchanged for the enemy, but the enemy and the stranger both reveal the monstrous nonetheless. We can also link Bain's feeling of unfamiliarity with herself to the theme of unfamiliarity with home and our earlier discussion of "going back."

At the end of the film, Bain repeats her previous remarks with a slight modification: "There is no going back to that other person, that other place. This thing, this stranger, she is all you are now." Bain's understanding of her own transformation, which turns her into a thing, a stranger, a monster—positioning her elsewhere—is key, for it places the stranger/monster within a particular setting. Bain is not the same person, for instance, because New York is not the same city. When confronting her fiancé's killer, who had taken the couple's dog during the attack, she demands, " I want my dog back!" in the way someone might remark, "I want my life back." In other words, "I want things restored to the way they were." While this restoration is not fully possible, the enacting of revenge works to stabilize Bain's world. When facing the second of her assailants, who called Bain "bitch" during the assault and renamed her stolen dog "Bitch," Bain asks, as she shoots him, "Who is the bitch now?"

CONCLUSION

The three films discussed above channel some of the anxieties developed by Americans after the events of September 11, 2001, and packaged by the *9/11 project. Flightplan, Lakeview Terrace,* and *The Brave One* can all be conceptualized as 9/11 films, both in relation to their release dates and with respect to the issues central to their plots. These films develop the discourse and ideologies of the *9/11 project* without specifically addressing the events of September 11, 2001, and in the case of *The Brave One*, by creating a 9/11 allegory. By so doing, the films explore American anxieties in the wake of a changed America, including how Americans might respond to and ultimately cope with a perceived world in which terrorists will always find ways to launch attacks regardless of government action and, perhaps relatedly, with an expanding array of 9/11 monsters. These films likewise begin to question viewers about how far they would be willing to transform themselves in order to protect themselves and their loved ones. The fact that neither of the films offers a resolution regarding the transformation of the main characters tells viewers that this question is open-ended—it is one we are still exploring as a country.

Moreover, these films offer racialized and gendered lessons concerning the United States after September 11, 2001. These issues include matters of borders and boundaries as they engage with notions of American security and citizenship. All three films highlight instances in which the familiar—a plane one designed, the neighborhood in which one lives, a city one thinks one knows—transforms into a source of fear and threat. The individuals in these films must take matters into their own hands, fighting various "monsters to destroy." As Chernus elaborates, "Monsters are not real—unless you believe in them. Monsters exist only in fictional stories. But if you really believe in the stories, you will believe in the monsters. Then the monsters will have very real effects. That's how monsters become real" (Chernus 2006, 1).

Flightplan highlights the uncertainty or ambiguity of threats, as it simultaneously questions taken-for-granted understandings of reality. The film conveys to audiences that no one is safe under any circumstances and that protectors can pose a threat to one's safety and security as readily as more typical monsters. Pratt and her family suffer the consequences of a world in which people are not able to easily discern threats, where they are not able to trust authority, and where authority dismisses one's insecurity or reveals itself as the actual source of that anxiety. The only recourse a person might have, in such a context, is to blow up the monster after it is revealed. However, with this solution comes a transformation of one's self—a transformation into someone or something unrecognizable and (ironically, perhaps) itself monstrous.

Lakeview Terrace presents a scenario in which places that should offer security (one's neighborhood, one's home) reveal themselves as both physical and psychical battlegrounds. The film suggests that there is no safe haven and, like *Flightplan*, implies that an authority figure and person assigned to one's safety and security might unleash a monster instead—a monster living next door, within one's presumed safe environment. Importantly, one is transformed into something unsettling and unfamiliar in contending with this monster. And while external threats might receive a sort of resolution within these films, the enemy/stranger/monster within continues beyond the final scenes of these 9/11 movies.

The Brave One posits a certainty to threats and proposes that some actions might be justifiable in response to them, even if those actions (because of their horrific nature) irrevocably change the individual actors themselves. Bain is transformed into an avenging monster herself. Even more unsettling, she comes to understand what she has become and knows there is no way back to her former self. This irrevocable change parallels the change that Americans see for themselves in the wake of September 11, 2001—a day that changed America forever. Within this storyline, viewers witness an unfolding of the Bush narrative and its continuing impact on a United States still very much affected by the *9/11 project*. The suggestion is that threats are everywhere, and a heightened state of vigilance is required in the face of this America—an America that becomes changed, we might add, partly via one's response to and construction of those 9/11 monsters.

In concluding, we would like to briefly address the gendered portrayals in these films. We've pointed out, through films discussed in previous chapters, that white American men are the epicenter of action and reaction in a 9/11 context. We addressed the fact that in many 9/11 films, especially those dealing with the events of September 11, 2001, or the wars issuing from these events, white American men are portrayed as those facing and managing the insecurities and burden arising from such a deeply impactful moment. In this chapter, we've addressed two films with white American women as lead characters (interestingly, played by the same actress). In both cases, viewers see the characters burdened with defending themselves and those they love from the threat of 9/11 monsters. The main character in the chapter's third film, also defending himself and his family, is, not unexpectedly, a white man.

Although the three lead characters find themselves in similar predicaments fighting threats and enemies, we can identify a fundamental difference between them: Mainly, the women (Pratt and Bain) must ultimately transform themselves into something unfamiliar, while the man (Mattson) acts in a more (stereo)typical manner. The transformations that occur unfold as the films proceed, and they are lasting in shape and impact. While Mattson also undergoes a fundamental change, this change does not appear permanent; in the end, he does not kill anyone. Both Pratt and Bain must be aggressive, and different from Mattson, they must kill in order to accomplish the immediate resolution of both plots. Mattson, though willing to consider this possibility, is given a reprieve as others neutralize the threat for him. Mattson is not asked to step outside his role as a white American man—a man who procures help from others in managing his burden. While the depth of the changes to all characters remains unresolved at the end of these films, it is clear that Pratt and Bain have undergone full metamorphoses, whereas Mattson might have been spared a permanent alteration.

Chapter Five

9/11 Transnationalism and Gendered Citizenship

Nationalism . . . does not emerge out of one imaginary community but rather is produced through the changing specularity of consumer culture and contingent community affiliations created by new and historical hierarchies of race and gender and which extend beyond the boundaries of the nation-state. (Grewal 2003, 536)

In 2011 a Gallup poll showed that for 53 percent of Americans, "It was extremely important that the government take steps to halt the flow of illegal immigrants into the United States" (Morales 2012). More generally, the poll showed that 64 percent of Americans "are dissatisfied with the level of immigration into the country" (Morales 2012). In a survey conducted by the Pew Research Center two years later, 41 percent of Americans interviewed agreed with the statement, "Immigrants today are a burden on our country because they take our jobs, housing and health care" (People Press.org 2013). In June 2013 a CNN/ORC International Survey showed that 62 percent of Americans thought that when it comes to immigration policy in the United States, "border security should be the main focus" (CNN.com 2013).

At the same time as Americans expressed concern to contain an increasing number of incoming bodies, secure the border, and minimize impacts of specific bodies already here, they also seemed intent to explore the world. According to a 2012 LivingSocial survey, "78% of Americans have visited at least one other foreign country and 36% have traveled to four or more foreign destinations" (Jernigan 2012). However, travel for Americans, as with most other endeavors, is also gendered. As recent numbers on the travel advice website *The Gutsy Traveler* convey, 70 percent of travel decisions, including booking cruises, group travel, tours, and tickets, are made by women. This percentage rises to 92 percent when online travel purchases are added. Moreover, women comprise 75 percent of those who take cultural, adventure, or nature trips. And perhaps more telling, 87 percent of women travel to places "for the beautiful scenery," compared to 72 percent of men (Bond 2012).

The numbers cited above present an important aspect of the 9/11 United States and *9/11 project*: Borders are constructed as open in one direction only. Taken together, both sets of statistics show the dissonance in perceptions regarding non-American bodies moving *in* versus American bodies moving *out*. The fact that American bodies, and other First World bodies in general, can transcend international borders with ease and entitlement is at the heart of the *9/11 project* and the films analyzed in this chapter.

FIRST WORLD SUBJECTS AND PERMEABLE BORDERS

As part of (re)inventing white masculine citizenship, developing ideologies, creating monsters, and rewriting history, the 9/11 racial and gendered framework reflected in Hollywood films (re)creates the world—especially the world extending beyond U.S. borders—as an uncontained, frightening, and unpredictable space for white American and/or European citizens. The space, however, is one that these citizens must nonetheless occupy. That is, as productive of fear and anxiety as this uncontained and unpredictable world might be, it does not deter central characters in mainstream films from traveling abroad or trying to save global "others." In fact, the 9/11 Hollywoodized world tends to reveal no borders for First World peoples who appear to own and readily traverse the globe. Americans and First World citizens in general are physically able to cross, and to symbolically transcend, national boundaries with ease. In so doing, they become transnational citizens of sorts, while maintaining their national markers or citizenships.

The story for non-First World citizens is a different one, as the film industry maintains strict divisions for them. Perhaps reflecting Americans' views on migration and travel, filmic borders are permeable in one direction only. Within 9/11 Hollywood films, the citizenship or national background of individuals becomes entangled with their gender and the space they are allowed to inhabit, typically determining their fate within the narrative. In the case of American or First World citizens, regardless of whether they are in Europe, Southeast Asia, or Africa (that is to say, regardless of "where in the world" they are), they are vicarious ambassadors of the American/First World way of life. As Inderpal Grewal conveys, after September 11, 2001, "foreign policy and economic power [are linked] to the moral and secular discourses of democracy, rights and freedoms, and the patterns of work, leisure and consumption that insert the individual into the nation" (2003, 536). We would add to this statement, "and the globe." Additionally, the place a person occupies in the world of film becomes dichotomized as either one of salvation or damnation for the resident of the global North.

In this chapter, we examine the films *Babel* (2006), *Children of Men* (2007), and *Eat Pray Love* (2010) to illustrate various aspects of 9/11 filmic representations of First World citizenship, including its transnational and perhaps global aspects, which are always in service to whiteness and maleness. *Babel* offers a broad account of the world after September 11, 2001, especially as Americans have conceived this world, vis-à-vis issues of threat and security. While centering citizenship and the global flow of goods and bodies, *Babel* presents viewers with a world that cannot be contained and, thus, a world that threatens the security of white American citizenship. More tragically, *Children of Men* relates the conditions of a fictional world without children, which is to say, a world without a future. In this case, the threat of a world of nonreproducing adults is not only a threat to American and European citizenships but to all citizenships. This world is enveloped by chaos, which is why the white European protagonist resolves to save a black immigrant woman, who is pregnant. Viewers are to think that by saving the woman, he is saving the future of the human species and humanity itself. However, as we discuss below, saving the future comes at the expense of the present, and the protagonist must sacrifice his life in the process of saving the woman and her baby. *Eat Pray Love* tells the story of a white American woman using the world at her disposal to save herself from herself by searching for feelings and insight. The plasticity of the world in *Eat Pray Love* serves as a backdrop to her search for meaning, and American citizenship serves as her passport. In the end, she finds not only herself but also love by exploring the world—possible due to the fluidity granted by her American citizenship. All three films feature versions of 9/11 First World citizenship—a citizenship granted to white American and European bodies and one that becomes useful in making sense of and perhaps transcending a newly revealed chaos. This type of citizenship encounters trouble in the uncontained world, but it overcomes obstacles and attempts to save and/or redeem itself and others in the process. Thus, it keeps true to the precepts of the *9/11 project*, including its wars, the militarization of key aspects of society, renewed nativist efforts, new air-travel protocols, and a highly racialized and gendered ideology.

As previously discussed, after September 11, 2001, governmental rhetoric began to link perceived outside threats (Muslims; countries harboring terrorists) with perceived inside ones (immigrants; same-sex couples). This linking projected the United States as a vulnerable place and Americans as a vulnerable people—both in need of vigilant state protection (Bloodsworth-Lugo and Lugo-Lugo 2010). Consequently, at the same time as the country was experiencing a massive expansion in the capabilities of its communication technologies, linking people in the United States with others in every corner of the globe, the U.S. government was instituting the Department of Homeland Security (DHS)—one of the more far-reaching and pervasive federal agencies ever to be created in the country. The self-imposed mission of the department was to "secure the nation from the many threats it faces" (Department of Homeland Security 2010).

With relentless efforts to secure the nation and its people, ideologies surrounding open access and closed borders began to coexist, some of which are exemplified by the polling results discussed at the start of this chapter. As Americans were getting in touch with people around the world via their computers and electronic devices, the DHS was intent on containing the nation and its people, equating containment with security and protection (Bloodsworth-Lugo and Lugo-Lugo 2010). It is no coincidence, then, that the Immigration and Customs Enforcement Office (ICE), in charge of monitoring who enters the United States, surveying its borders, and deporting undocumented immigrants, is under the purview of the DHS. Paradoxically, as these elements of the *9/11 project* were put into place, Americans were developing a renewed appreciation for travel.

BABEL: THE UNCONTAINABILITY OF THREATS AND
REACH OF U.S. CITIZENSHIP

Efforts to contain and protect Americans after the events of September 11, 2001, have been portrayed in several films, including
Babel, that question and perhaps challenge the effectiveness of this
effort by providing viewers with a narrative of constant global and
local threats to American citizenship. Juan Pellicer states that *Babel*
"illustrates with didactic eloquence the dynamics of film poetics
generated by transtextuality and montage and also by the creative
and harmonic correspondence between signified and signifier, content and expression, story and discourse, cinema and verse, and by
the fortunate relation between the drama of the structure and the
structure of the drama" (2011, 248–49). While we pay close attention to "the drama of the structure" here, more important than its
aesthetic value, to us, is the fact that *Babel* offers a capsule containing significant clues involving First World fears about Third World
subjects in an era characterized by an ongoing War on Terror.

Overplaying the permeability of national borders for American
citizens in *Babel*, Mexican director González Iñárritu presents
viewers with a somewhat frightening link between life outside of
U.S. borders and certain aspects of life in the United States. He
does so by deploying the clichéd notion of the human web, or six
degrees of separation, on a global scale. The film suggests that
American citizenship, or perhaps more to the point Americanness,
is transnational in nature and operation, and it shows viewers the
weight this carries globally. This is done by taking viewers through
seemingly disconnected events in the lives of several people on
three continents: namely, Africa, Asia, and North America. As the
plot unfolds, viewers see that regardless of how far these characters
are from each other physically, their lives (and fates) are indeed
connected in meaningful ways. And they are directly affected by
each other's actions and positionalities. However, it is not the "we
all live in a small world" message that is important to the present

discussion but the theme to which the characters bear witness—namely, the uncontainability of the world. This uncontainability hints at the impossibility of any office of the American state, regardless of its global reach and efforts, to keep its citizens safe and secure—whether inside or outside of its borders. In the world *Babel* presents to viewers, American citizenship is fragile and at the mercy of Third World subjects, brilliantly illustrating the 9/11 racialized and gendered frame.

The film begins in a yet to be identified desert with people speaking Arabic and a bartering negotiation occurring between two men, Abdullah (Mustapha Rachidi) and Hassan (Abdelkader Bara), who are exchanging a rifle for money and a goat. Viewers soon learn that the rifle is for Abdullah's young sons, Ahmed (Said Tarchani) and Yussef (Boubker Ait El Caid), to use against jackals that threaten the family's herd of goats. Once the exchange unfolds, the sons take the rifle to watch the goats, and in an effort to determine how far the rifle can reach, Yussef, the younger son, ends up shooting at a bus full of tourists. One of the bullets critically wounds Susan Jones (Cate Blanchett), a white American female tourist who is in the country with her husband, Richard (Brad Pitt), trying to sort out some difficulties in their marriage. It is after Susan is wounded that viewers learn this part of the story takes place in Morocco.

As the film continues, the plot moves to a suburb of San Diego where Amelia (Adriana Barraza), a Mexican nanny, is in charge of Mike (Nathan Gamble) and Debbie (Elle Fanning), two white American children whose parents appear to be out of the country. Viewers listen in on a call from the children's father (Amelia's boss) who tells Amelia that he was not able to find anyone to watch the children, so she has to stay with them longer than anticipated. Amelia raises the fact that it is her son's wedding day and that she needs to be present at the wedding, which will take place in Mexico. In light of the situation, her boss commands that she reschedule the wedding, volunteering to pay for a "new one." After Amelia is unable to find an alternative arrangement, and being unwilling to reschedule her son's wedding, she takes the children to Mexico with her.

After immersing viewers in Amelia's predicament, the plot moves to Tokyo, Japan, where Cheiko (Rinko Kikuchi), a high school girl, is playing volleyball. Viewers quickly learn that Cheiko and her teammates are deaf. As the plot unfolds, it becomes clear, through her interaction with men, that Cheiko is desperately seeking attention and closeness. Prompting, or perhaps compounding, her behavior is the fact that she and her father, Yasuhiro (Koji Yakusho), are struggling with the recent death of her mother. It is clear that the mother's absence represents an open wound of sorts for Cheiko, making her prone to anger and frustration. Cheiko is also dealing with her father's detachment.

The story lines in the film unfold in a variety of languages, and the inability to communicate and lack of understanding are principles moving the plot; hence, the film's title. But the 9/11 undertones are what bring the entire film together. For instance, after Susan is shot in Morocco, the incident is treated and investigated as a terrorist act by both the Moroccan and American governments. Not knowing it was one of his sons who had shot the American woman, Abdullah discusses the incident with his wife over dinner, telling her that according to authorities, a terrorist shot the woman. Abdullah's wife's response is both swift and telling: "But there are no terrorists here." The investigation leads Moroccan authorities to Hassan, and eventually to Abdullah and his sons, after Hassan tells authorities that a Japanese hunter had given the rifle to him as a present, and he (Hassan) in turn sold it to Abdullah. In fact, once it is determined that Abdullah was the last owner of the rifle, he and his sons are chased, and Moroccan police kill Ahmed.

Back on the North American continent, although Amelia is able to cross the United States–Mexico border to attend her son's wedding with the American children without difficulty, on her way back, she encounters trouble. We can recall, here, that the permeability of the First World runs in one direction only. Amelia's nephew decides to run from authorities, and this decision puts her life and the lives of the two children in danger. At this point, viewers learn that these are Susan and Richard's children. In the end, Amelia is deported back to Mexico, even though she explains to the immigration official in charge of her case at the detention center that she has worked in the United States for the last fifteen years, rents a house in San Diego, and has taken care of the two children since they were born. Finally, viewers learn that the rifle sold to Abdullah by Hassan, fired by Yussef and wounding Susan, was given to Hassan by Yasuhiro, Cheiko's father. As Japanese detectives investigate the origin of the rifle, viewers are to infer that it was the same rifle Cheiko's mother used to take her own life, and this is perhaps the reason why Yasuhiro gave it to Hassan.

In addition to the shooting of Susan by a Muslim child in a Muslim country, the investigation of the rifle incident and the incident at the United States-Mexico border place *Babel* squarely within the context of a 9/11 film, as it portrays almost all aspects of the *9/11 project*. The film depicts the multiple, if inadequate, security efforts led by the American government involving the protection of both its borders and its citizens. And while there is no direct invocation of the USA Patriot Act, and not a single American soldier is present in the film, the presence of 9/11 and the War on Terror are nonetheless palpable—driving the international incident as well as the aftermath caused by a simple rifle exchanging hands.

CHILDREN OF MEN: CHAOS WITHOUT A FUTURE AND 9/11 AS A GLOBAL TRAGEDY

Directed by Mexican Alfonso Cuarón, *Children of Men* presents an end of the world scenario. Although it takes place in a dystopian

Britain in 2027, it is clear from the start that the film portrays a 9/
11-inspired setting, as it extrapolates from the events of September
11, 2001, to the entire world by presenting an extreme version of
what could happen if a global catastrophe were to occur. The film
begins with snippets of news coverage using a vocabulary that has
become quite familiar within the United States and other First
World countries after September 11, 2001: "Muslim communities
demand a cease of the occupation of mosques," "The Homeland
Security Bill is ratified," "After eight years, British borders remain
closed," and "The deportation of illegal immigrants continues." As
the film develops, viewers learn that the last person born on Earth
was "Baby Diego," who had been born in Argentina in 2009. After
this time, humanity had endured 18 years of infertility. Within this
scenario, London is portrayed as a city within a military state, with
soldiers occupying the streets and guarding fenced-in refugee
camps and transfer stations. The images Cuarón presents are reminiscent of German cities during the Holocaust, Israeli checkpoints
near Palestinian settlements, and detention centers for undocumented immigrants in the United States after September 11, 2001.
This creates a type of historical continuity of images.

Early in the film, the main character, Theo (Clive Owen), makes
his way through the chaos that has become London and into a
coffee shop for his morning drink. As he exits the shop, he stops to
spike his coffee and a bomb goes off, lending an anxious 9/11 tone
to the film. While buying his coffee, Theo and the other costumers
attend to a television news story about Baby Diego being killed in a
bar brawl the night before. This piece of news affects everyone
negatively, as viewers see people glued to their computer screens
and television sets, mourning and crying over images of Baby Diego. Theo, who exhibits behaviors of a functioning alcoholic, seems
completely detached from what is happening around him. He appears resigned to the fact that within a few decades humanity will
cease to exist. Viewers realize that although people are dealing with

the lack of a future in various ways, Theo's apathy is fairly wide-spread and is randomly punctuated throughout the film. One of these random examples occurs when Theo is listening to the radio in his car, and the disc jockey makes the following point before playing, *Wait* by The Kills: "And now one for all the nostalgics out there. A blast from the past all the way back to 2003, that beautiful time when people refused to accept that the future was just around the corner." Theo's apathetic mood changes, however, after his ex-wife Julian (Julianne Moore), an underground activist, asks him for a favor. Initially, the favor involved securing fake documentation to transport a young woman to the coast. Reluctantly, Theo agrees to get the paperwork in order, but he must accompany the young woman himself.

As the story develops, and Theo makes his way through the city, viewers receive glimpses of the new British totalitarian government, which offers a response to and restructuring of a collapsing world. As with any other totalitarian regime, this one maintains power by utilizing two particular tools: the military and propaganda. Viewers are privy to two revealing pieces of governmental propaganda, both of which are constantly displayed on public transportation. One claims that "the world has collapsed" and "only Britain soldiers on," with images of chaos in various parts of the world. The other urges Britons to "report all illegal immigrants" and maintains that "employing, harboring, or feeding" any immigrant will be considered a criminal act. The extreme concern with illegality serves as an explanation for the soldiers on the streets, who are typically seen in front of fenced-in areas with immigrants contained behind them. Britain soldiers on by keeping such immigrants at bay. Samuel Amago conveys that by allowing viewers to experience the propaganda along with the characters in the film, Cuarón is using a filming technique that draws viewers in as he presents his view of the future (2010). The dystopic future the director envisions, Amago suggests, is informed by our political and ideological present. In his words:

> As co-viewers (along with the film's characters) of the various audiovisual stimuli that saturate the film's mise-en-scène, we are drawn into the dystopian world envisioned, so that our own perspective on events resembles that of the characters. This self-reflexive emphasis on media and representation can be related to the director's overarching concern with the politics of the present and how they inform the way we imagine the future. (2010, 213)

The plot becomes more complicated after Theo meets Kee (Clare-Hope Ashitey), a young woman who is an African refugee, and he learns what is so important about transporting her to the coast. She is pregnant, and they will meet a ship that will take her to the Human Project, an alleged underground research group in the Azores rumored to be attempting to end infertility. In an effort to protect her from the British authorities, Theo takes Kee to an old friend's secluded house. The friend, Jasper (Michael Caine), welcomes them into his home, and Kee learns that Theo and Julian had had a child, Dylan, who died during the flu pandemic of 2008. Kee and Theo are forced to flee Jasper's house after the authorities arrive in search of them. Jasper is killed, but Kee, Theo, and Kee's companion Miriam (Pam Ferris) are able to escape and contact an immigration officer—a meeting Jasper had arranged. The officer takes them to a refugee center with access to the sea. After many obstacles, including helping Kee to deliver her baby, Theo is able to place Kee on a boat. Theo, who is shot in the process, dies as the ship—blatantly named "Future"—approaches.

Although it presents an unreal situation (the possible extinction of the human race via global infertility), *Children of Men* builds its momentum by referencing, expanding, and linking its storyline to very real ideologies embedded within the *9/11 project*. The news clips at the start of the film set the tone by using a language with

which viewers are all familiar: Muslims, mosques, homeland security, illegal immigration, and closed borders. The omnipresence of
the military is reminiscent of images seen from Iraq, Afghanistan,
and the United States-Mexico international border. The fact that
Kee is a black "illegal" immigrant should not be taken lightly in the
development of the story. And the fact that she appears to have
been a prostitute before she got pregnant is also relevant. While
they are at Jasper's house, Theo and Kee have the following exchange:

Theo: Who's the father?

Kee: I'm a virgin. [She then laughs]. That'd be wicked, eh?

Theo nods.

Kee: Fuck knows, never learned half the wankers' names.

A black prostitute refugee from Africa provides viewers with a
simultaneous look at the past and the future of humanity. Human
life is supposed to have originated in Africa, and according to *Children of Men*, life would recommence thanks to Africa. The fact that
Kee has (and by extension viewers have) no idea as to who the
child's father is becomes a way of acknowledging humanity's ob-
scure beginnings. The Biblical references of both Theo and Miriam's names provide the film with a religious grounding and continuity in the narrative of humanity's origins. However, it is the non-
religious tropes of race, illegality, and hyper-surveillance that give
the film its decidedly 9/11 flavor. Amago points out that *Children
of Men* can be seen as "a manifesto in which Cuarón alternately
indicts the global political status quo while envisioning a brave new
future for the film medium" (2010). That which Amago calls an
indictment of the global status quo we see as a critical portrayal of
the *9/11 project*, including its ideologies and sensibilities.

EAT PRAY LOVE: 9/11 TRAVELING CITIZENSHIP AND PROJECTIONS OF GENDER

Eat Pray Love is clearly our most opaque reference to a 9/11 film. However, we maintain that its opacity renders it useful for further demonstrating that even without a direct link to September 11, 2001, or its aftermath, the reach of the *9/11 project* extends to unlikely places. Although initially set in New York City, the film never refers to the September 11, 2001, events, the ensuing wars, or any governmental agency created to manage the aftermath of that day. The film also lacks metaphors directly referencing 9/11 vocabulary or ideas. Nonetheless, we can note that embedded within the film is a 9/11 sensibility, to keep with Melnick's position discussed earlier in this project, as well as a portrayal of ideologies contained within the *9/11 project* discussed throughout.

Based on a memoir, *Eat Pray Love* relays the story of Liz Gilbert (Julia Roberts), a New Yorker who must travel to various parts of the world so she can "learn to feel" again. Although *Eat Pray Love* offers a somewhat similar message of connectedness to that found in *Babel*, Liz's story and the film's narrative depart from the questions raised in the former by deploying a First World fluidity of citizenship that allows her to travel wherever she pleases (specifically, to countries starting with the letter "I"). Through this fluidity, Liz can move from New York City to Italy, India, and Indonesia (Bali) in her quest to feel once more.

The film begins with Liz's narration of an experience with her friend Deborah, a psychologist, when she was asked to offer psychological counseling to Cambodian refugees. According to Liz's narration, Deborah was "daunted by the task," wondering how she could "relate to their suffering" or "help these people." In the end, Liz conveys, all they wanted to discuss with Deborah was their love problems:

I met this guy in the refugee camp. I thought he loved me but when we got separated on the boat, he took up with my cousin. Now he says he loves me and keeps calling me. They are married now. What should I do? I still love him. What should I do?

Liz's conclusion is, "this is how we are." She then relays this message when meeting a medicine man on her first trip to Bali. She could have asked for anything she wanted, but in the end, all she wanted to ask about was love. Thus, viewers are led to conclude that when Liz sets out to feel again she means she wants to feel *love* again—even though she is married at the film's start.

Once the plot settles back in to New York City, viewers learn that Liz is not happy in her marriage. When she contemplates her options, she remarks, "the only thing more impossible than staying was leaving." Viewers also learn that Liz is unaccustomed to praying (she calls it "such a foreign concept"), conveying that as she was trying to pray for the first time in her life, she "almost began with 'I'm a big fan of your work.'" Once she leaves in search of rejuvenation, she lands in Italy, where she learns to eat guilt-free and start searching for a word that describes her. She uses "writer," but as someone else indicates, that is what she does, not who she is. Liz also discovers by visiting the Augusteum in Rome that "ruin is the road to transformation."

From Italy, Liz moves to India, where she tries to find peace by doing selfless, devotional work. She tells Richard, whom she has met there, that she feels more disconnected than ever. Her outlook about life and meditation changes when she gains the insight that "God dwells within you as you." This discovery provides the peace she has been seeking and helps her to make the final move in her journey—back to Bali in Indonesia. While in Bali, Liz reconnects with Katut, the medicine man. She meets new people, including Wayan, whom she helps gather enough money through friends to build her own house. At one point, Liz conveys that had she not come back to Bali, she would not have come back to herself. She meets her new love and finally finds the word to describe her: attraversiamo—which she translates as "let's cross over."

Liz's self-discovery is hardly interesting, especially compared to the cultures, nations, peoples, and borders that she must engage and transcend in order to gain insight into her own life. But it is the ease with which she is able to use the globe as therapy that brings *Eat Pray Love* within the fold of a 9/11 film, as it illustrates the global reach of U.S. citizenship. The film lacks other elements discussed at the start of this chapter; however, it does posit that First World citizens belong in the world, while Third World citizens belong within the constraints of their national borders. Liz is able to move through nations, but Third World subjects (in India and Indonesia) stay very much confined within the borders of their own countries.

Moreover, Liz's travel presents a different side of First World citizenship from the understanding offered by the two previous films, shedding light on the masculinity that overpowers those films. Mainly, at the same time that Liz's First World citizenship provides her with an unlimited pass allowing her to travel the world without minding borders, her travel is exclusively for self-discovery and self-improvement. Her endeavors are incredibly narcissistic, for although she does try to help a few women in the countries she visits, this can be considered part of her main goal of being able to feel again. Thus, she is placed in a different position from the main male characters in the previous two films, who also travel but are doing so for more noble causes. For instance, Richard tries to strengthen his marriage in *Babel*, and Theo sacrifices himself to save the world's future in *Children of Men. Eat Pray Love* thereby conveys much to viewers about white masculinity and femininity in a 9/11 world.

We might add one final point about Liz's character in *Eat Pray Love*. Given certain parameters, she can serve as a metaphor for America. Mainly, Liz's insights, as she tries to find herself, are indicative of the uncertainty and chaos that has become 9/11 America. While this might not be the intent of the director, or the author of the original book, it does seem to be a reasonable metaphor given that Liz's crisis is portrayed in a world after September 11, 2001, and by an American character. *Eat Pay Love* author Elizabeth Gilbert conveys, "Happiness is the consequence of personal effort. You fight for it, strive for it, insist upon it, and sometimes even travel around the world looking for it." As with films discussed in previous chapters, certain resolutions must often be sought abroad, given a troubling and unfamiliar American landscape. While certainly very different from soldiers returning to war, the travel taking place for Liz and Susan (in *Babel*) is done to effect a result impossible to find at home: achieving happiness or repairing a marriage respectively. We return in chapter 8 to the gendered meanings associated with the different forms of leaving home and acting in the world; mainly, one that is individualistic and self-interested, and another that is for a greater good or cause even when one's personal conflicts are involved.

CONCLUSION

The films discussed in this chapter reflect important ideological nuances operating in our 9/11 world that invoke specific racialized and gendered aspects of citizenship. These films convey that Hollywood films after September 11, 2001, project American and European (First World) citizenships as white and affording access to the entire world. However, white male citizenship and white female citizenship have different roles and goals, suggesting that the race and gender of these characters is not irrelevant for they embody certain ideologies as their bodies convey specific messages about the 9/11 world to viewers of the films.

In *Babel*, Richard's whiteness serves as a symbol of, or a cautionary tale to, white Americans when he decides to travel outside of U.S. borders and delegate the primary care of his children to an

undocumented immigrant. Such decisions render Americanness un-
safe. Filmmakers have taken lessons from U.S. history, showing
that these messages are best delivered through a white, male character. In the case of *Children of Men*, Theo serves as surrogate for
all white men in the First World. He must relinquish his privileged
position and allow the world to continue without him. But first, he
must ensure that the world *will* continue without him. This becomes
the ultimate redemption for white men, perhaps lending resolution
to the white male insecurity, vulnerability, and burden created by
such a catastrophe. Here, the reality of the September 11, 2001,
events lurks in the background, even though the film highlights
instead an unrealistic human scenario. In *Eat Pray Love*, Liz's
character serves as a complement to white, male First World citizenship in that it is precisely her citizenship that allows her to use
the globe as a therapeutic tool. While white female citizenship
might be fragile (recall Susan being shot by a Moroccan child and
Julian having to live a clandestine life), it nonetheless extends its
reach well beyond American shores. In so doing, it provides a
counterpoint to non–First World citizenships broadly speaking, as
well as to the highly visible, take-charge citizenships of white
American/First World men after September 11, 2001.

It is also worth noting that the directors of *Babel* and *Children of
Men* are Mexican nationals, and the fact that they are able to portray specific elements of the *9/11 project* so deftly speaks to the
pervasiveness of these ideologies. These two non-American directors are able to capture and portray both the infrastructure and the
ideologies of the project, even in films that are neither fully based
in the United States (*Babel*) nor in the United States at all (*Children
of Men*). Finally, and returning to Grewal's point in the chapter's
opening epigraph, the most important aspect of these films is that
they manage to construct specific nationalisms by positioning the
main characters, both physically and metaphorically, outside the
borders of their respective countries. And perhaps more hauntingly,

the ideologies that reside behind their bodies carry specific 9/11 messages to viewers in the United States and across the globe.

Chapter Six

Animated 9/11 Raciality and Conceptions of Progress

> As quintessential forms of American public culture, animated movies may be examined as a site where collective social understandings are created and in which the politics of signification are engaged. (Giroux 1999, 2)

In 2006 the Pew Research Center released the results of a survey showing a sharp downturn in "personal optimism" since 2002—the sharpest in the more than forty years that both Pew and the Gallup organization had been conducting this survey (Taylor, Funk, and Craighill 2006). According to the report, the survey

> employs what researchers call a "self-anchoring scale," where respondents are first asked to give a numerical rating to their present quality of life. Then, having "anchored" themselves in the present, they are asked to rate the past and future the same way. They are not asked if they think the future (or past) is better or worse. They are simply asked, in succession, to rate three points in time on the same numerical scale. (Taylor, Funk, and Craighill 2006)

Americans' tendency is to rate their present above their past but below their future, suggesting that they have expectations of linear progress (from worse to better) in their lives. In fact, according to the researchers at the Pew Research Center, "At any given moment, the public as a whole believe they were worse off in the past and will be better off in the future, [suggesting] a blissful state of constant human progress" (Taylor, Funk, and Craighill 2006). Given the results of this particular survey, however, the researchers concluded that since 2002 "some of the edge has come off good old American optimism" (Taylor, Funk, and Craighill 2006). And given the year, the perceived decline in optimism can be explained, at least in part, by the traumatic events of September 11, 2001.

To put the survey results into further perspective, 49 percent of respondents in 2006 expected to live better lives in five years. This marks a decline when compared to 2002, when the number was 61 percent. While in 2002 only 7 percent of respondents expected their lives to be worse in five years, that number rose to 12 percent in 2006. Both of these percentages are still relatively small. The researchers also point out that the results are affected by race, as "blacks and Latinos are more likely than whites to forecast personal progress for themselves" (Taylor, Funk, and Craighill 2006). The same is also true for "younger adults, college graduates, and people with higher incomes" (Taylor, Funk, and Craighill 2006).

An important aspect of this survey is its global component; it was administered in forty-four countries and covered all inhabited continents. The results from the global elements shed some light on Americans' optimism and notions of progress, as "[the American public was] more inclined to say it had made progress than were the publics of any country surveyed in Europe or the Middle East and most of the countries surveyed in Asia, Latin America and Africa" (Taylor, Funk, and Craighill 2006). The high numbers showing Americans endorsing a consistent positive outlook, both in absolute and relative terms, should not be surprising, since Americans have been taught a history of progress involving their country and people, interwoven with the ideology of manifest destiny and personal tales of people pulling themselves up by their bootstraps. The overarching idea is that regardless of where we currently are, "we've come a long way." These narratives have created the imperative of progress, discussed in chapter 1, in relation to race and gender. In the end, it is whiteness and maleness that motivates and illustrates the narratives.

ANIMATED FILMS AND 9/11

As discussed throughout, the G. W. Bush administration dubbed the War on Terror emerging after September 11, 2001, "a new kind of war"—a war fought by the ultimate purveyor of democracy against countries fostering terror and harboring terrorists. In a similar way, after its release in 1995, movie enthusiasts began to refer to *Toy Story* (John Lasseter, 1995), with its computer-generated images, as "a new kind of animated film" (Robertson 2011). The majority of this "new kind of animated film" has been released after September 11, 2001. However, despite the claims, we can note that neither the War on Terror nor these more recent animated films are actually *new* (see Bloodsworth-Lugo and Lugo-Lugo 2010, 10). Although computer graphics, and more recent reliance on 3-D technology, might have created more vivid and malleable characters and lifelike settings, just like war, the stories these films tell (that is, their ideological components) are often the same stories historically told to children.

Having said this, the lens for these stories has been modified from earlier stories, as 9/11 animated feature films employ subtle constructions of the American vs. non-American dichotomy discussed in previous chapters, casting the American as the embodiment of progress, freedom, and individuality. In essence, these films tell powerful old stories through an equally powerful but updated frame. Dichotomized constructions involving Americanness include tropes alluding to, but never naming, "progress"—

whereby progress is presented as a linear process advancing in one direction. Within this structure, the present is always better than the past, and the future will be better than the present. The category "American" is presented as developed (that is, an accomplished and finished product) and is juxtaposed to the category "non-American," which is presented as a process still in development.

These films are decidedly 9/11 in their articulation of progress, not because they necessarily juxtapose democracy against terrorism, but because they deploy notions similar to those articulated by former President Bush regarding Americans looking forward to and embracing progress. Progress, thereby, equals democracy. Although terrorism may not be present in these films as such, the films do show threatening others that are 9/11 in their projection. Different from threatening others in earlier animated films, which present an immediate threat to the main character(s) exclusively, 9/11 threatening others poses a broader threat—a threat to progress itself. In *Planet 51* (2009), this threat is manifest as a threat of time period or era; in *The Princess and the Frog* (2009), the threat is one of race and gender relations; and in *Rio* (2011), the threat is extinction.

Perhaps because they are meant for children, these films typically portray the American vs. non-American dichotomy through simplified tropes and ideas. For instance, the quaint setting of chilly Minnesota is contrasted with the exotic, warm setting of Brazil in the film *Rio*. Representations of the exotic are of special significance, since they are often set in the global South and include questionable or strange customs that are used to contrast and reinforce conceptions of home—what's "ours" and what's familiar. Ironically, these films tend to deglamorize the exotic settings by rendering them problematic, while glamorizing life in the United States by oversimplifying it. By so doing, they support an idea of the United States as advanced and other locations as undeveloped. This lack of development, in turn, is part of what makes other people and places foreign, in many instances underscoring their threat.

At times, the American vs. non-American dichotomy is portrayed via a time period removed from the present. *The Princess and the Frog*, set mostly in the 1920s, presents a clear example. Here, a problematic and highly undeveloped past is set against an idyllic and ideological notion of a righteous present—the moment in which viewers are living. These depictions, though remarkably sanitized, suggest to American viewers that we have indeed come a long way. The dichotomy is sometimes more complicated in construction, placing linear and familiar stories of progress within an "alien" setting. The plot of *Planet 51* provides such an example. Animated films deploying these stories advance ideological assumptions concerning what it means to move forward as a society, as well as what it means to belong to a society at all. In the United States after September 11, 2001, they reinforce particular constructions of Americanness, contrasting the American with the foreign or enemy other.

These films likewise portray specific aspects of the *9/11 project* in relation to culture and citizenship, and they advance certain conceptions about race that, while not necessarily the result of 9/11 ideologies, are specific to and constitutive of animated films for children. Often, painful stories about race are either rendered invisible or folded into the story lines of animated films in ways that make them both irrelevant to the stories being told and subservient to particular formulations of citizenship. The story lines of these films recreate aspects of race and ethnicity without attention to the context within which these aspects have developed and been perpetuated. More to the point, they reveal race and racial distinctions without racism or the institutional measures creating those distinctions in the first place. Elisions of race in animated films operate in tandem with 9/11 notions of citizenship and societal/cultural progress privileging these while neglecting racial and historical inequalities. These films rely on an American vs. non-American dichotomy to present circumstances, events, and desires as simply human, ahistorical, and universal, rather than as white, contextual, and American.

As Thomas McCarthy has noted, far from being devoid of racial meaning, ideologies about progress and development (which he calls "developmental schemes") designate groups that "have been represented not only as racially distinct but also as occupying different stages of development, with their degree of advancement often being understood to depend on their race and to warrant various forms of hierarchical relations" (2010, 1). Far from being mere and innocent forms of entertainment, animated films also channel racism as "teaching machines," in the words of Giroux, inspiring "at least as much cultural authority and legitimacy for teaching specific roles, values, and ideals [as] more traditional sites of learning" (quoted in King, Lugo-Lugo, and Bloodsworth-Lugo 2010, 8). This point is especially relevant when we consider that through learning, racial categories and categories about citizenship are created and perpetuated, racial and racist hierarchies remain in place, and ideologies of progress and categories of mutual exclusion are constructed. The lessons viewers receive from animated films work to maintain these racialized, hierarchical, and ideological constructions—including constructions about citizens and others—resonating with and validating certain understandings of the world.

In this chapter, we consider *Planet 51*, *The Princess and the Frog*, and *Rio*, their notions of race, and their 9/11 messages regarding progress and the American vs. non-American (that is, the threatening other) dichotomy. In the case of *Planet 51*, notions of progress are attached to an alien species living on an alien planet, in what appears to be a version of a moment in U.S. history—the 1950s. Through the intertwined notions of alienness and past U.S. history, a particular story of progress is told. Viewers, especially

American ones, are also prompted to understand developmental schemes. Through the film's presentation of aliens, viewers see a different "race" (or species), but also reflections of themselves in the past—a past less sophisticated than the present, replete with superstition and erroneous belief. Returning to the poll discussed at the start of this chapter, in the eyes of Americans, this is a past "worse off" than the present day.

Similarly, *The Princess and the Frog* employs narratives regarding the past to invoke notions of progress and Americanness. By retelling a princess story (albeit a *black* princess story) from a racially segregated time and space within U.S. history—but without directly pointing out this fact in the film—Disney positions the U.S. present in relation to its recent past, one that was also "worse off." Different from other Disney fairy tales involving princesses, however, the story of this princess and frog takes place, not "once upon a time" in a fictional land "far, far away," but in a real setting: 1920s New Orleans, Louisiana. Through this actual setting, viewers are encouraged to measure progress and development in relation to race—and to a great extent rewrite history in the process. *Rio* weaves a narrative of progress in relation to Americanness through animated animals. With a bird as its main character, *Rio* tells a tale of white American citizenship and belonging—one punctuated by a sharp contrast between bland Minnesota and exotic Rio de Janeiro. This contrast underscores the division between "us" and "them" reiterated throughout the Bush presidency and the *9/11 project*, and it positions viewers to experience the contrast between the familiar and unfamiliar.

PLANET 51: SEA MONKEYS, RACE, AND CONCEPTIONS OF (WHITE) CITIZENSHIP

Historian David Roediger claims, " The idea of race . . . emerged and continued to have meaning amid evolving processes in which

government, economy, and society sorted peoples into very different relationships to property, to management, to punishment and to
citizenship, according to fictive biological categories" (2005, 212).
Such embeddedness within structures that sort and allocate place-
ments in society via perceived biological differences can lead to
similar understandings in other contexts, such as what might happen when encountering an alien species in an alien world. In *Planet
51*, a white male American astronaut, Captain Charles "Chuck" T.
Baker (Dwayne Johnson), does just this when he lands on an unfamiliar planet and firmly plants the U.S. flag into ground he pre-
sumes he is the first to encounter. Instead of being alone, Captain
Baker encounters "little green people"—the natives or inhabitants
of the planet.

Upon first meeting, the natives and Captain Baker regard *each
other* as aliens. This categorization reinforces mutual mistrust,
which is captured in the following exchange between Lem (Justin
Long), a Planet 51 native, and Captain Baker:

Lem: You were just talking alien.

Captain Baker: Hey, I'm not the alien here. You are.

Lem: Me? You are.

Captain Baker: No, you are.

Lem: You are. You . . . you came to my planet.

Captain Baker: An alien planet. Hello.

The mutual alienization that occurs between Lem and Captain
Baker is presented as a funny exchange between two individuals
upon first encounter. But the presentation of this exchange clearly
glosses over the fact that there is no level playing field in such
encounters, since the captain, as a representative of a culture seem-

ingly more advanced and knowledgeable than Lem's, poses an impending threat to Planet 51's inhabitants—that of invasion and conquest. The captain's planting of the flag is reminiscent not only of space operations viewed by all Americans on television, but also of colonizing missions and militarized invasions, including perhaps the invasions of Iraq and Afghanistan and ensuing wars. Captain Baker's obliviousness is also telling, for as Lem's side of the exchange suggests, the captain is the actual alien or foreigner on Planet 51. The fact that Captain Baker does not understand this, viewing Lem and his people/planet as alien/foreign, points to Captain Baker's United States/Earth-centric "we came, we saw, we conquered" perspective.

Eventually, Lem and Captain Baker overcome their differences through friendship; however, the trajectory to this endpoint is significant for discussions of race and progress in the film. Prior to Captain Baker's landing on Planet 51, viewers learn that the "aliens" living there exist in a less advanced state than "we" do. In fact, they appear to be living in a 1950s, suburban, America-like setting with two-story houses and white picket fences in neatly kept neighborhoods where everyone knows and barbecues with their neighbors. The residents have aspirations similar to those promoted through notions of advancement embedded within rhetoric of the American Dream. For instance, after securing a new position as assistant curator at the planetarium, Lem tells his friends, "Hey, I can see my whole life: A house, a car, two kids. They'll grow up and have kids. They will come home to visit us on holidays." The residents even speak English, as Captain Baker discovers shortly after landing and encountering Lem for the first time.

Viewers likewise learn that the inhabitants of Planet 51 have a rather primitive understanding of the universe. While lecturing and guiding children, as the new assistant curator at the planetarium, Lem remarks, "Thanks to science, we now know the universe is nearly five hundred miles long, and it contains, you're not gonna believe this, over one thousand stars. And still, the only known intelligent life is right here on our planet." This understanding could be interpreted as a parody of viewers' own ideas about the universe, and even mainstream Americans' own perceptions of themselves. However, Lem's interpretation is later dispelled, when Captain Baker sets the record straight:

> Captain Baker: See that star, the little red one? Circling that star is a planet called Earth. It's about twenty billion miles away. Give or take.
>
> Lem: There's no way space is that big.
>
> Captain Baker: What? Are you kidding? There's billions of galaxies. And each galaxy has billions of stars. Next to that, kid, our planets are just dust in the wind.
>
> Lem: So, nothing I knew was right?

This exchange conveys the perspective from which the story in Planet 51 is told. It indicates that there is an accurate and inaccurate, progressive and outmoded, and right and wrong understanding. Captain Baker represents intelligence, while Lem displays ignorance. By extension, Earth (or America) is enlightened, and Planet 51 is backward.

Supporting their lack of sophistication is the fact that inhabitants of Planet 51 are terrified of, and obsessed with, a possible alien invasion. Aliens, they believe, would turn them into zombies. They appear simultaneously horrified and fascinated by this prospect. Repeated references to alien invasions occur in the film, along with scenes depicting inhabitants' fears. It is within this culture, fearful of alien invasions and zombie impacts—reminiscent of the fear of Communists in the United States during the 1950s—that Captain Baker finds himself. Authorities, who believe he has come to transform Planet 51's inhabitants into zombies, target Captain Baker as a threat. The film recreates Albert Memmi's notion of the historical figure as "the stranger/outsider." Memmi states, "The outsider provokes a malaise that involves both distrust and respect. The stranger could be the incarnation of the devil or a deity in disguise. In either case, whether a joyous event or the onset of the plague or a windfall for one and all, it is best to be vigilant" (2000, 72). Of course, in *Planet 51*, "the stranger" could be either Captain Baker or the inhabitants of the planet, given the way that historical context is erased.

The conflict between Captain Baker and the inhabitants of Planet 51 extends beyond concerns over alien invasion. He is presented as an astronaut of our time, as illustrated by an iPod found in his rocket and references to such things as being on Facebook and desiring a frappuccino. In fact, these are the only referents for any sort of culture clash between the American astronaut and the Planet 51 inhabitants. The primary clash between them can be viewed more as a matter of time difference than of culture. That is to say, Captain Baker's references to contemporary items would have garnered the same bewildered reactions if he traveled back in time to the 1950s United States. However, from the start of the film, various remarks can be interpreted as biologizing difference—not merely grounding that difference in time or culture. For instance, Skiff (Seann William Scott) offers bathroom instructions to Baker as follows, "If you have to do a number one, use these papers [Skiff has placed newspapers on the floor]. If you have to do a number two, go outside. And, if it's number three, I can't help you." In another instance, when seeing Captain Baker naked, Skiff comments to the others in the room, "That's a funny place for his antenna." Other comments and exchanges focus on levels of attractiveness and the inability to determine such matters in a foreign environment. When offering Lem encouragement about Neera (Jessica Biel), his love interest, Captain Baker says, "I mean, look at her, lose the antenna, get some plastic surgery, she's a hottie."

These exchanges are intended to be comic, of course, but they also serve to highlight just how physically different Captain Baker is from these "creatures." They may speak English, live in cute houses surrounded by white picket fences, listen to '50s music, and have similar dreams; however, viewers must remember, they are still "little green men" or, perhaps, not *men* at all. When trying to determine what went wrong with his mission, Captain Baker remarks in frustration, "It's supposed to be uninhabited, not full of sea monkeys dancing to the oldies." This description of Planet 51's inhabitants provides, perhaps, the film's greatest insight. Viewers are privy to the exasperation the astronaut is feeling, which leads to his name-calling. The use of the term "sea monkeys," though intended to have a comedic effect, should actually make viewers pause, since it is being used in the same way as other insults; for example, porch monkeys, sand jockeys, and wetbacks. Memmi conveys, "The temptation of racism is the most commonly shared thing in the world" (2000, 129). The producers of *Planet 51* extend the scope of Memmi's point, suggesting that the temptation of racism extends to other places in the universe—especially if an American "explorer" is involved. Moreover, epithets are a way of othering a group, and since September 11, 2001, the process of othering groups deemed threatening has included the U.S. government working to contain these people and countries. While the characters in *Planet 51* do not represent a threat to humans yet, Captain Baker has begun the process of othering by creating a epithet for their group.

At the end of the film, as Captain Baker prepares to leave, he tells everyone, "You're a great planet, and your '50s are fine, but give me a call when you get to the '60s, 'cause that's gonna be fun." The idea that Planet 51 will develop in a linear fashion and replicate the U.S. historical trajectory is telling, and viewers can actually see elements of the '60s already taking shape as Neera and Glar (who resembles a California surfer dude, drives a VW van, and sings an adapted Bob Dylan tune) spend their free time protesting for " the cause." However, it is worth noting that Captain Baker's characterization of the '60s as fun, as well as the erasure of racism and racial segregation in the 1950s Planet 51 setting, suggests that these time periods have been sanitized in the story of progress. While an expectation of advancement has been established, undesirable aspects of the so-called advanced stages have been elided—for example, wars, assassinations, social unrest, and inequality. These elisions are, perhaps, made more palatable through the deployment of Dwayne Johnson—Black Canadian and Samoan—to voice Captain Baker, a decidedly white American character. This insertion has similarities to the use of male characters of color in the service of whiteness addressed in chapter 1, although here, it occurs via the astronaut's overt appearance. The issue of white domination is minimized through the voice of a person of color.

THE PRINCESS AND THE FROG: RACE AND PROGRESS IN THE WORLD OF DISNEY

In *The Princess and the Frog*, Tiana, Disney's "first black princess," is actually a waitress who is accidentally transformed into a frog in her quest to become a restaurant owner. Princess Tiana (Anika Noni Rose) differs from other Disney princesses in several respects, the most obvious being the fact that she is black. However, beyond Tiana's groundbreaking blackness is the fact that she is introduced as a little girl in a home with two loving and available parents. In fact, unlike in other princess stories, it is her father, James (Terrence Howard), and not her mother, Eudora (Oprah Winfrey), who eventually dies—although he does not die before informing viewers of how much he loves Tiana and passing on to her his dream of owning a restaurant. Another departure from other Disney princess tales involves the film's setting. Different from "a time long, long ago" and "a land far, far away," Tiana is positioned within a definite and concrete time and place: 1920s New Orleans. In addition, Tiana has dreams of her own (albeit borrowed from her father) that extend beyond wishing to be rescued from an awful and unfair life. Tiana's life, though certainly difficult and full of hard work, does not seem awful or unfair, even though—in virtue of the film's setting—she is supposed to be living in a segregated United States that considers and treats her as less deserving than the whites around her.

Within the film, notions of progress are portrayed through Tiana's longing to own a restaurant, and her working and saving toward this dream, which—as noted above—is an extension of her father's (unfulfilled) dream. Viewers learn, through a musical vignette, why James was not able to fulfill his dream: He was killed prematurely during World War I. James's death allows Disney to avoid pursuing a story line involving a black man attempting to open a restaurant in segregated New Orleans. The impossible dream is placed on the daughter, who is able—within the princess narrative—to transform first into a frog, and then into a princess, before finally managing to own a restaurant. Importantly, she comes to own the restaurant only through the help of, and her association with, nonblack characters such as Prince Naveen (Bruno Campos) discussed below. The father's death, via war, also gestures to a situation experienced by many children and families with family-member soldiers in harm's way after September 11, 2001.

The process through which Tiana achieves her dream centers our analysis here, since the film, overall, elides the genuine structural hardships that a black woman living in Jazz Age New Orleans would have faced in pursuit of this dream. The deep segregationist practices in place at the time are displaced in favor of less conventional—or simply, fictional—hardships (for example, voodoo mag-

ic and transformation into a frog). The real hardships that Tiana
faces are, in fact, portrayed as based on social class and not race:

Tiana [groaning]: It serves me right for wishing on stars. The
only way to get what you want in this world is through hard
work.

Prince Naveen: Hard work? Why . . . why would a princess need
to work hard?

Tiana: Huh? Oh, I'm not a princess. I'm a waitress.

Prince Naveen: A waitress? Well no wonder the kiss did not
work! You lied to me!

Tiana: I—I never said I was a princess.

Prince Naveen: You never said you were a w–waitress! You
were wearing a crown!

Tiana: It was a costume party, you spoiled little rich boy!

Thus, New Orleans, birthplace of Plessy v. Ferguson, becomes not
a Jim Crow place, but a place where notions of hard work are
tested—a place where American conceptions of pulling oneself up
by one's bootstraps are rearticulated. Excluded from this presentation of social class are historical connections to race, racial hierarchies, and development.

Viewers also see, within *The Princess and the Frog*, that Tiana—as a frog—spends her time attempting to escape the difficulties of the bayou. The lesson here is clear: There is the city and
there is the swamp; whereas the city is a place in which dreams
might come true, the swamp connotes (white, " hillbilly") ignorance and (black) magic—a backwardness that must be escaped in
order to advance. Throughout the film, Tiana repeatedly advocates

hard work as the only means of achieving her dream. Her blind trust in hard work is another inheritance from her father, who conveys this lesson to her when she is a little girl. Later, as Tiana contemplates her life as a frog, she makes the following resolution: "I worked hard for everything I got and that's the way it's supposed to be. When I'm a human being at least I'll act like one. If you do your best each day good things are sure to come your way. What you give is what you get! My daddy said that and now I'll never forget." Mama Odie (Jennifer Lewis) reinforces this message by telling Tiana, "You are your daddy's daughter. What he had in him you got in you." She tells Tiana to dig a little deeper and then asks whether Tiana understands the message. Tiana responds, "I need to dig a little deeper and work even harder to get my restaurant."

Tellingly for the story line, the first time Tiana vacillates on this conviction, she is turned into a frog. The second time, at a winner-takes-all encounter with voodoo doctor Facilier (Keith David), she manages to escape doom by sticking to her convictions. The exchange between Tiana and Dr. Facilier occurs toward the end of the film, when she is holding his talisman, which he wants back:

Dr. Facilier: Gotta hand it to you, Tiana. When you dream, you dream big. Just look at this place! Gonna be the crown jewel of the Crescent City. And all you got to do, to make this a reality, is handle that little talisman of mine.

Tiana: No. This—this is not right.

Dr. Facilier: Come on, darlin'. Think of everything you sacrificed. Think of all those people who doubted you. And don't forget your poor daddy. Now, that was one hard working man . . . double, sometimes triple shifts. . . . Come on, Tiana, You're almost there.

Tiana's aspirations to own a restaurant had been delayed when her realtors, the Fenner Brothers, informed her that a man had outbid her and paid cash for the property—an old sugar mill—that she desired. Within the exchange between Tiana and the Fenner Brothers (Jerry Kernion and Corey Burton), we note the only indications in the film that Tiana is a black woman living in the Jim Crow South, and that this is how others perceive her. Viewers are momentarily placed outside of Disney's enchanted world, and into Tiana's segregated one, when one of the brothers hints that this turn of events is perhaps for the better, since "a little woman of [her] background would have had her hands full trying to run a big business like that." The politeness of these words is sheer Disney, but the meaning transcends its typical magical world, affording a hint of the reality of what Tiana's daily life must have been like. Although what part of her background the realtor intends (a waitress? the daughter of a seamstress? a young person? poor?) is never clarified for viewers, we can assume that being black must be part of it. The "little woman" component of the comment, to which we return below, adds to the importance of the statement, for it offers a decidedly sexist overtone and not a racist one. This seems the most Disney is willing to offer in underscoring the life of a young black woman living in the 1920s South.

The fact that this is the only indication Disney provides that the production team for *The Princess and the Frog* is aware of the context in which they are developing the story is not surprising nor is the individualized way with which sexism is presented and racism is elided. Disney has always omitted certain aspects of reality. However, the film's explicit setting in a defined historical place and time—one that would, in reality, foreground sexual and racial inequality—renders this elision particularly troubling. Moreover, while the realtor does acknowledge Tiana as a woman, this is more likely a reflection of the time during which the film was made (the start of the twenty-first century) than of the time during which it took place (almost a hundred years earlier). The amorphous context within which the acknowledgment is placed generally undermines its impact. It is Tiana's condition as a woman, within a general remark concerning her "background," that makes her unsuitable for the endeavor of owning a piece of property.

Of overall significance to the message of *The Princess and the Frog* is the fact that Tiana's dream of restaurant ownership is ultimately made possible through her marriage to Prince Naveen. While the film's explicit references are to hard work and individual achievement through due diligence, the main character's goal is actually—finally—realized through proximity to privilege, power, and resources. Tiana's father, as a black man within a particular U.S. history, could neither achieve his dream of restaurant ownership nor could he offer Tiana material support for doing the same. It is only through her association with an ambiguously raced figure (Prince Naveen's racial identity is never clearly marked, and his place of origin, unlike Tiana's, appears to be fictional) that Tiana advances from the societal position held by her father. Note the following exchange:

Prince Naveen: I have to do this and we are running out of time!

Tiana: I won't let you!

Prince Naveen: It's the only way to get you your dream!

Tiana: My dream? My dream wouldn't be complete . . . without you in it. I love you, Naveen.

Prince Naveen: Warts and all?

Tiana: Warts and all.

While this dialogue incorporates Naveen into Tiana's success, it would be more accurate to say that the fulfillment of Tiana's dream would actually not be possible without Naveen.

RIO: BLUE BIRDS AND WHITE AMERICAN CITIZENSHIP

Rio begins in the Brazilian jungle, showing viewers birds beginning their day by singing and dancing samba, until smugglers begin to trap and put them in cages. One of the caged birds is a baby blue macaw, which ends up in a cold, snowy place (named in the film as "not Rio"). As a little girl, Linda ends up rescuing the baby blue macaw, names him Blu, and a photomontage shows that they grow up together. Viewers learn that as adults, Linda (Leslie Mann) owns a bookstore, and she and Blu (Jesse Eisenberg) have a nice, tranquil life together in "not Rio," which turns out to be Minnesota. Blu appears to enjoy the comforts of being a domesticated companion bird, which, as he conveys, includes the perfect marshmallow-to-cocoa ratio: six marshmallows to a cup.

The perfect, tranquil life that Linda and Blu enjoy is changed when Tulio (Rodrigo Santoro), a Brazilian ornithologist, pays them a visit, conveying that Blu is the last male member of his species. Tulio wants them to come to Brazil so Blu can mate with the last known female member of the species before the entire species is gone. At first, Linda refuses to go, but then she has a change of heart and convinces Blu that going is the right thing to do. She adds the promise, "We will be back before you even know it." Linda and Blu arrive in Brazil during Carnaval, and she and Tulio have the following exchange as she is trying to make sense of the commotion:

Linda: What's going on?

Tulio: You arrived in time for Carnaval.

Linda: Carnaval?

Tulio: Yes. It's the biggest party in the world. You know, a time to have fun and dance.

In the meantime, Blu is having a conversation of his own with two local birds, Pedro (Will.I.Am) and Nico (Jamie Foxx). The first thing he tells them is, "I am not from here." When he conveys that he is there to meet a girl, the birds offer him advice; Pedro says that he must "keep things spicy."

Blu finally reaches his destination and meets his prospective mate, Jewel (Anne Hathaway), who is intent on escaping their enclosed space. A "half-witted gang of smugglers" kidnaps Blu and Jewel, and the birds find adventure escaping from the smugglers. Escape is made difficult by the fact that they are chained together and that Blu can't fly. They also have differing goals, as Blu wants to go back to Linda and Minnesota, and Jewel wants to be free in the jungle. In the process of escaping, they meet Rafael (George Lopez), a toucan, who tries to teach Blu how to fly by telling him that flying is done not with the brain but with the heart. Rafael states, "And when you feel the rhythm of your heart, it's like samba. You fly." Blu learns to fly at the very end of the film after he has fallen in love with Jewel and must rescue her from the smugglers—showing that flying is indeed done from the heart. He brings her to Linda and Tulio so they can fix a wing she broke while trying to escape, and we learn through a musical montage that Blu and Linda stay in Brazil, where Blu and Jewel have three baby macaws. Linda and Tulio also adopt Fernando, an orphan child who helped them find Blu after he and Jewel were kidnapped.

The film presents viewers with a colorful depiction of Brazil, its people, and its Carnaval. Depictions of Brazilians in the film are fairly straightforward. According to the film, Brazilians party hard (in costumes) and watch soccer on their television sets. Because it is a film for children, it presents a highly sanitized picture of the country, eliding the brutal realities of orphanhood, contraband exotic animals, and life in the favelas, even though they are all present in the film. The film also presents an interesting take on transnational adoption, even if it is done by way of a bird. The first thing Blu says is, "I am not from here," when in fact he was born and first opened his eyes in the Brazilian jungle. Similarly, leading to the climactic scene of the film, Blu gets angry at Jewel and tells her and Rafael, "I don't belong here. I never wanted to come here in the first place, and you know what? I hate samba!" Blu's lack of connection with his place of birth is striking, as it tells us he is used to the comforts of the American way of life. The fact that he was raised in the country's heartland transforms him into a white American bird.

The contrast between Blu's embodiment of white Americanness and the fauna he encounters in Brazil is also important, not only because the majority of these characters are voiced by actors of color (except for Jewel, interestingly), but also because they talk with certain affectations and cadences associated with people of color *in* the United States. Although Brazilians voice many of the human Brazilian characters, nonwhite Americans voice three of the main Brazilian animals (Nico, Pedro, and Rafael). The fact that children watching the film can recognize familiar nonwhite accents in the global South is important, for these voices serve as reminders of what is not American. This is why the casting of Eisenberg, a white American actor with no discernible accent, as Blu's voice, is key, as Blu continues to claim he is not from "here" when in Brazil and finds the place to be "not-Minnesota," constantly pointing out things that seem different and scary.

The film offers viewers an important lesson in the American vs. non-American binary, for it is in the sharp contrast between the global North and the global South that we see the *9/11 project.* The contrast of familiar, quaint, tranquil, and snowy Minnesota against the exotic, colorful, and sweaty landscape of Rio de Janeiro—with

its Carnaval and soccer-obsessed inhabitants—provides a clear il-
lustration. But it is the lesson in progress that offers the most insight, for the film does not simply contrast the global North and the
global South, it also places the South as an area whose places and
inhabitants must be explored, rescued, and saved. It is also an area
contributing to the extinction of Blu's species, and we do not have
to turn that into a metaphor to understand its implication: the global
South is a threat to progress in the global North.

In the case of *Rio*, the North-raised protagonist chooses to stay
in the South where he was born and make a life and raise his
offspring along with his loved one. Linda also chooses to stay and,
along with Tulio, has adopted Fernando and created a wilderness
preserve. The choice they make in the name of progress (by saving
an orphan child and the blue macaw species) is a testament to the
unstoppable reach of white American citizenship, which can overcome the constant fiesta spirit of Brazil and create a space for more
sensible living. Minnesota, standing for the United States and the
global North more generally, still remains the measure of progress
against which Brazil's quirkiness and threat is compared. This is
why throughout the film viewers see constant reenactments of this
dichotomy. Here are a few examples: Linda is almost forced to eat
rooster; no one understands the phrase "cheese and sprinkles" when
Blu uses it as an example of two things that go well together; and
Linda is asked to "shake her tushi" during Carnaval, to which she
responds, "We don't shake our tushies in Minnesota." The clash of
customs and cultures is used as a way of pointing out how long the
road to progress will be for Brazil.

CONCLUSION

Similar themes in *Planet 51, The Princess and the Frog,* and *Rio*
underscore elisions of race and 9/11 notions of Americanness and
social/cultural progress. In relation to progress, they all show or

suggest a linear model of advancement, whether on a societal level or a personal one, in much the way that respondents to the survey discussed at the beginning of this chapter do. In the case of residents of Planet 51, these are positioned as residing in a less advanced time, although they are expected to progress to the next presumed stage—from the time period of the 1950s to that of the 1960s, both as lived within the United States. Moreover, certain perceived undesirable aspects of these decades—specifically, problematic race relations and racism—are omitted altogether. Yet the representation of a fictional planet with references to inhabitants as alien and backward promotes a view of the other as less advanced and inferior, mimicking views about people of color held by whites in a variety of historical contexts. It also positions white Americanness as the more evolved of the two races—a race/citizen that should be both emulated and followed.

In *The Princess and the Frog*, a black man is unable to achieve his dream of restaurant ownership, while his black daughter—the next generation—is able to fulfill the same dream. This marks a classic example of linear progression. However, despite explicit references to hard work, it is more so Tiana's connection to an advantageously positioned light-skinned man that affords the dream's fulfillment. Through eliding racial segregation and structural disadvantage, Disney avoids confronting realities of race and racism in the 1920s or present-day United States.

Such omissions are significant and problematic, since, as McCarthy states, "A factor at work in sustaining neoracist responses to racial stratification is the invisibility of the historical causes of existing racial imbalances. Historical unconsciousness of institutional racism in the past feeds unconscious neoracism in the present" (2009, 89). While some might claim that matters of race and racism should not be addressed within the confines of a children's film, neglecting such issues puts into place the mechanisms for continued disadvantage and in fact underscores racial—and perhaps, racist—messages. This is especially problematic in the case of a film set in an actual time and place, even if it is a princess tale. Perhaps more importantly, the little that the film does offer in relation to race provides viewers with enough information to draw their own inferences about progress: Things today are better than they were back then—a pat-on-the-back truism meant to demonstrate that the stages of social development in the United States have meant we are going in the right direction.

The elisions of race and representations of progress and Americanness in *Rio* keep with these traditional representations. Using the Carnaval and soccer as defining features of Rio, and thus of Brazil and Brazilians, the film is able to traipse viewers through orphanhood, the favelas, and animal contraband in a way that seems almost negligible but, even more importantly, disconnected from *our* lives. These are presented as situations that take place in the global South, indicating how far behind they are from the progress made in the global North and how different the people in these areas are from the people in *our* part of the world, even if certain individuals from our part of the world decide to live their lives "down there."

The importance of animated films for children, as noted by Giroux, is that they instruct and help socialize children by presenting digestible versions of ideas and ideologies. When these films present viewers with certain elisions of race, and when they pair those elisions of race with 9/11 ideological constructions of Americanness and progress, these films teach children ideas about themselves and others. It is in the mix of these representations, and their ability to teach lessons, that we find the strength of racial representations alongside the *9/11 project* and 9/11 ideologies.

Chapter Seven

The Great Recession and White Masculine (In)Security Again

Many of these guys may be great on the back nine but totally lack the skill set to get them through anything like this. If you went to the college of your choice, married the woman of your choice, and bought the house of your choice, you've never dealt with rejection. You've never had to develop fortitude. If not quite the Great Depression, it is certainly the Great Humbling—Judith Gerber. (Marin 2011)

During uneven economic times since the early 1990s, especially when a recession has seemed possible, Gallup has asked Americans the following question: "How likely do you think it is that there will be a recession in the country during the next 12 months—very likely, fairly likely, not too likely, or not at all likely?" In October 2007, 40 percent of Americans reported thinking that a recession was "very likely / fairly likely," while 57 percent said it was not too likely / not at all likely" (Carroll 2007). When asked whether the economy was already in recession, 58 percent said that it was not (Carroll 2007). While not depicting an overwhelming majority, a year before the 2008 stock market crash, a relatively high percentage of Americans seemed to anticipate an economic downturn. This perception was amplified by financial standing, as 51 percent of respondents with less than $50,000 in annual income thought a recession was very or somewhat likely, while only 33 percent of those with more than $50,000 in annual income thought the same.

In a poll conducted approximately a year later, Gallup found the lowest self-evaluation for standard of living by Americans (Brown 2013). The standard of living index is a measure of perception and self-assessment, through a ratings system, of Americans' satisfaction with their current standard of living and estimation of whether it is getting better or worse (Brown 2013). Although Americans began 2008 with a 36 percent standard of living index, by October it had plunged to 14 percent, the lowest registered in the five years Gallup had been measuring it, from 2008 to 2013. The results of both polls combined showed Americans to be very aware of the impacts that changes in the economy would have on their lives. Dubbed the Great Recession, the extent of the economic woes of 2008–2009 was unprecedented in recent history, so it is not surprising that Americans were quite wary of their own (economic) futures. For instance, another Gallup Poll showed that in October 2009, 46 percent of workers worried that their benefits would be reduced, 32 percent worried that their wages would be reduced, 31 percent worried that they would be laid off, and 27 percent worried that their hours would be cut back (Saad 2013). These were the highest numbers registered since Gallup began asking such questions in 2003. The economic collapse of 2008 emerged as a major event for the American public, adding to Americans' already existing fears and anxieties around threats in the wake of the September 11, 2001, events.

In this chapter, we argue that public discourse, including film narrative, around the Great Recession and its catastrophic global impacts continued to underscore 9/11 ideological notions of protection, security, and the containment of threats within the United States as embedded within the *9/11 project*. We propose that the Great Recession, and especially the economic downturn marked by the stock market crash of 2008, was a unique event—especially for white American men. While not disconnected from other economic collapses in American history, it was also tied to the specific social and political phenomenon of 9/11. As with any significant event that impacts American life, the Great Recession occurred within a very particular sociopolitical context, informing how the event itself has been viewed and experienced.

Historians and economists have drawn notable parallels between the Great Depression of the 1930s and the most recent economic meltdown, anchoring their discussions within the regular and irregular ups and downs of a capitalist economy. Tim Worstall's 2010 essay for *Forbes* magazine, "The Great Recession Is Just Like the Great Depression," provides an example. Although we understand the importance of establishing these parallels, we maintain that the way the Great Recession has been articulated and handled by the general public and social/political pundits and institutions sheds more light on where we were as an American society at the end of the first decade of the new millennium than about our economic history as such.

Thus, we contend that the Great Recession must be discussed within the context of 9/11 politics and ideology, the core of which has been dominated by preoccupations with a discourse concerning inside and outside threats. In fact, a quick Google search reveals that the Great Recession has been characterized as a tangible yet amorphous threat, similar to the threat of terrorism after the events of September 11, 2001. Both have an identifiable point of origin, but the repercussions and ramifications of each appear without end. In addition, when news articles, blogs, and other social media sites discuss the Great Recession, they typically conceptualize it as posing a threat to some*thing* (such as the airline industry, the middle class, or even the country itself) or some*one* (such as home owners, young adults, or baby boomers). The Great Recession has been articulated as a threat to the United States' economic order and, by extension, to American citizens and Americanness itself.

Several films released during 2010 and 2011 capture the idea of the Great Recession as a threat to various aspects of Americanness. Even more interesting, these films focus on a specific kind of threat posed by the Great Recession—the threat to white male masculinity. In fact, even when women are present, and even when people of color are included within the plots, the stories told by these films present viewers with white American men either affected by or dealing with the economic downturn. Viewers see these men struggling to cope with and survive a shifting landscape. These films tend to outright glorify white maleness and earnestly lament its failings during the recent global recession. To illustrate this pattern, we analyze four films: *Up in the Air* (2009), *The Company Men* (2011), *Wall Street: Money Never Sleeps* (2010), and *Larry Crowne* (2011). Similar to films portraying the events of September 11, 2001, addressed at the start of this project, the films included in this chapter create a narrative around white male American citizenship in which "American" is depicted as being endangered and in need of reconstitution or reinvention. In this regard, these films highlight themes addressed throughout the book while providing a slightly different cast to the *9/11 project*.

FILMS (NOT) ABOUT THE ECONOMIC MELTDOWN

Before we begin our film analysis proper, we would like to highlight a further connection between and among these four films: that is, even though they are all situated within the context of the 2008 economic collapse or its aftermath, all four directors strenuously claim *not* to have made films about the event. In a review for the *New York Times*, Joe Nocera conveys that according to *Wall Street: Money Never Sleeps'* director, Oliver Stone, "The [economic] crisis was merely meant to be the backdrop for a story about a handful of 'complex' people—an older, wiser Gordon Gekko among them—who just happened to be operating on Wall Street around September 2008" (2010). According to Nocera, Stone concluded, "People won't watch a business movie." However, of the four directors, Stone is the only one willing to acknowledge that his film was informed by the events of the Great Recession. In an interview with Amy Raphael for the *New Statesman*, Stone remarks, "When I started thinking about [the movie], I realized that the financial collapse of 2008 was the payoff for the 1980s. It was the culmination of a credit bubble of enormous proportions, where easy money was prevalent and people became really spoiled"(Gilbey 2010,73).

The other three directors were more reluctant to tie their films to the Great Recession, offering instead a transcendent message. We can note that this reluctance mirrors the reticence shown by directors to explicitly acknowledge the events of September 11, 2001, as informing or motivating their films, as we have previously discussed. In an interview with PopSugar Entertainment, and using language similar to that used by Stone, *Up in the Air* director Jason Reitman remarks that his film is not about the state of the economy at the time but that the economy serves as a background or metaphor. In his words:

> I never intended to make a movie about the economy. The economy doesn't interest me as much as [it's] just sort of a backdrop or metaphor for human connection, which was more important to me and that's what I wanted to tell a story about. But certainly as the world changed and we went from an economic boom to one of the worst recessions on record, I had to take it seriously and scenes that were originally humorous were scenes that I had to make authentic and real and dramatic. And that's why I started to use real people for people who've lost their jobs, people who actually lost their job instead of actors. (2009)

We can recall here the use of real people in the film *United 93*, discussed in chapter 2, for similar dramatic purposes and to promote authenticity within the film. In both films, real people were interwoven with actors to reflect the gravely serious human impact—even if the events behind the two films are also very different.

Similar to Reitman's claim that his film is based on happenings prior to the economic collapse, *The Company Men*'s director, John Wells, states for *Interview* magazine that he developed the film's script during a different economic event. He states:

> I wrote the script for Warner Brothers during the dot-com years. But by the time I turned it in, the recession was over, and no one wanted to see it. When things got rough again in 2007, I went back and looked at it. I talked to more people to make it more contemporary. Then [I] found out we were shooting it in the worst recession since the Great Depression. When we were shooting it, we thought we were going to release it as a historical document. "Here's what happened, and now we're all out of it." But [not quite]. (Mohney 2010)

Of the four directors, Tom Hanks appears the most adamant to avoid connections between the Great Recession and his film. In an interview with Roger Moore for the *Orlando Sentinel*, Hanks proposes that *Larry Crowne* was "going to be about the American propensity for starting over from scratch," and "the economy sort of caught up with it" (2011). And in an interview with Steve Weintraub, Hanks describes *Larry Crowne* as a battle against cynicism. He states:

> We are competing in a marketplace in which the thing we might have going for us is the true battle against cynicism. That's what *Larry Crowne* is about more than anything else. [A]t the end of this film, Larry Crowne lives in a crappy apartment. He still has a lousy job. He can't even afford to pay for the gas in his big car and he's going to school with no real set future of what's going to happen. But he's got this amazing new, forceful presence in

his life and he can honestly say, "The best thing that ever happened to me was getting fired from my job." (2011)

The firm claims by these directors not to have made films about the Great Recession is significant, for they suggest that the directors might be influenced by the events almost without realizing or understanding them, similar to everyone else. The claims also recall notions of national trauma discussed in chapter 2, and the attendant need of time for the American public to process such trauma before it can be (safely) projected onto the film screen. The directors' denials (to varying degrees) that the Great Recession frames their films perhaps helps to make them more palatable to American viewers still emerging from the effects of the Great Recession. This would be similar to concerns of it being "too soon" to depict the events of September 11, 2001, as we discussed in the case of *United 93* in particular. Regardless of their stated intentions, all directors seem quite capable of portraying the Great Recession and its tropes quite effectively, as we discuss below.

For the most part, the films reflect and convey both tacit and explicit ideas about the Great Recession as positioned within the *9/11 project*. Along with the turbulent economic terrain, the films portray unstated but significant lessons about race, gender, and Americanness consistent with viewers' experiences in the United States after September 11, 2001. Moreover, we are not alone in seeing connections between these films and the Great Recession, even if the directors might insist otherwise. In his review of *The Company Men* for the *New York Times*, Stephen Holden states that the film "powerfully revisits a theme touched on last year in the bitter comic drama *Up in the Air*: the devastating impact of sudden downsizing on corporate executives who have lived by the treacherous adage 'You are what you do'" (2010). Similarly, writing for *Entertainment Weekly*, Owen Gleiberman notes, "You know that feeling you got during the downsizing sequences in Up in the Air— the dread, empathy, and outrage mixed with the chilling sensation that anyone could be next, including you? That's the feeling that extends to every minute of *The Company Men.*" (2010).

We contend that this common theme among these films is not coincidental nor is the whiteness and maleness of the protagonists. Together, they convey a specific narrative regarding perceptions of (in)security, fragility, and resilience in the face of an unprecedented event—a narrative that extends beyond a mere economic lesson. Similar to the white men in films previously discussed in this book, the men in the films discussed here are vulnerable. They also carry a burden—a burden they must struggle to resolve.

THE COMPANY MEN: FRAGILE WHITE MEN AND THE GREAT RECESSION

In his review for the *Chicago Tribune*, Michael Phillips calls *The Company Men* "a tale of recessionary morals, ethics, and consequences" (2011). The film begins with television news scenes of the 2008 stock market plunge, squarely placing the film's opening scene at the start of the Great Recession. These images are followed by shots of a naïve and unsuspecting Bobby Walker (Ben Affleck), a man in his mid-thirties, preparing for work, driving his Porsche, and barging into a meeting bragging about his morning golf game. Bobby is fired within the first four minutes of the film, but his arrogance continues as he tells his wife, Maggie (Rosemary De-Witt), not to let anyone know that he is now unemployed. Bobby also wants to continue living above his means by remaining in his impressive near-million-dollar home, driving his sports car, and regularly playing golf at the country club. In fact, his overconfidence is so severe that when he begins attending an outplacement agency, he tells his cubicle mate, Danny (Eamonn Walker), that he [Bobby] will get a new job within a few days, even though Danny has already conveyed that he has been searching for months with no success.

In addition, Bobby yells at his wife when he finds out that she has cancelled his golf club membership. She tries to convince him that things are not how they used to be, saying, "This is real. This is happening to us," to which he replies, "I have to look successful." Bobby initially turns down an offer from his brother-in-law, Jack Dolan (Kevin Costner), in his construction business. And it takes him a full three months to begin to understand his predicament—long after his wife and children have accepted the situation and begun to make adjustments on their own. Bobby's slow realization of the unfolding situation links to the poll results at the start of this chapter, which suggested that those with higher levels of income were less likely to think a recession was likely. Once a recession actually begins, then, it is reasonable to think that these same people would be less likely to see it as occurring. Once Bobby finally does admit the situation and acknowledges that he has not gotten a single job offer during this time, he concludes, "I'm a thirty-seven-year-old unemployed loser." Viewers witness Bobby's original denial as a form of protection for his fragile self-image—an image based on work, money, and possessions. Not incidental to this image are Bobby's whiteness, maleness, and Americanness, which are in a similar state of fragility.

Viewers witness an even more heartbreaking vulnerability with Phil Woodward (Chris Cooper), Bobby's former coworker, who is sent to the placement agency when he is also fired. Phil is fifteen to twenty years older than Bobby, and viewers see him struggle to find a job due to his age. Phil ends up committing suicide, asphyxiating himself with carbon monoxide in his own garage after doing dishes and taking out the trash, but before this he has a conversation about his predicament with Gene McClary (Tommy Lee Jones). In this conversation Phil conveys his distress at not being able to afford his daughter's college tuition and the lifestyle to which his family has grown accustomed. He concludes, "The world didn't end. The newspaper still came every morning, the automatic sprinklers went off at six. Jerry next door still washed his car every Sunday. My life ended and nobody noticed." For Phil the loss of his job not only means a loss of livelihood, it also means a loss of identity and life. The world, for Phil at least, had indeed ended.

The fragility and vulnerability of these two men is tragic, but obviously, only Bobby remains to be redeemed. His path to redemption begins with *real* hard work (that is, manual labor), after his brother-in-law hires him to do carpentry. The work affords Bobby a means to regain the masculinity he had attached to his job and possessions, all of which are lost when Maggie sells his Porsche, they do a short sale on their house, and they move in with Bobby's parents. Jack and Gene (Bobby's former boss) keep Bobby grounded throughout the film. While Jack provides the opportunity for him to work with his hands (to literally construct something), Gene offers him a "second chance" (a start from the bottom to rebuild his confidence by "building" a new company). In fact, reiterating the "work with your hands" lesson, Gene tells Bobby that when the company they formerly worked for began, the workers labored with their hands and "knew who they were, knew their worth." Bobby is seen entering the modest new company floor at the end of the film, giving instructions to the office workers, and finally asking, "What's the worst they can do? Fire us?" Viewers see that Bobby has learned a lesson, overcoming the threat that unemployment posed for him by trading his arrogance for a healthier confidence.

But there is one more person to offer Bobby some solace during this ordeal—his cubicle mate, Danny, mentioned earlier—who is an out-of-work black engineer with a PhD. Bobby gets his brother-in-law to hire Danny in construction. However, at the end of the film, when Gene starts his new company and hires Bobby to run it, Bobby hires everyone who used to work with him and had spent the last few months at the placement agency—but viewers do not see Danny. *The Company Men* is the "whitest" of the films that we discuss in this chapter, and the fact that Danny's story is dropped at the end of the film tells viewers that the film, or perhaps more poignantly the Great Recession, is not about people of color. The idea of "working with one's hands" underscores notions of hard work and underlying connections to the mythology of Americanness, which continues to link white masculinity with being American. As we discussed in chapter 2, this mythology also places value on white masculinity in such a way that the rescuers on September 11, 2001, could not be envisioned as nonwhite. Again, characters of color in 9/11 Hollywood films serve supporting and/ or redeeming roles for white men—white men burdened with the aftermath of unprecedented and traumatic events.

In his review of *The Company Men* for *Entertainment Weekly*, Owen Gleiberman conveys, "This is one of those roles tailor-made for Affleck's fast-break charm, his ability to play a 'winner' cruising at too high an altitude" (2010). Gleiberman concludes, "The dialogue pings, and often stings. Yet *The Company Men* invites our compassion toward the men who glided along on a house-of-cards economy until it fell in on them, too" (2010). This is a telling statement, for these are white men for which viewers are supposed to feel compassion: Bobby for his naiveté and arrogance, Gene for his resilience, Jack for his spirit (viewers learn that he is losing money but does everything he can to keep his men employed), and even Phil who commits suicide after understanding that he is too old to find another job. The fact that Danny's story line is erased conveys a great deal about the way Hollywood directors view and understand the Great Recession, even when they precisely claim not to be making a film about it. It also connects the theme of recession to the themes of the *9/11 project*, which collectively underscore a type of white man's burden informed by the ideology of 9/11.

In his essay "No Company for Old Men," sociologist Bernard Beck maintains that the lessons from the film, however, are incomplete. In his words:

> Although *The Company Men* ends well, it does not resolve two big issues it raises, the burden of exaggerated masculinity in our culture of work and the return of a large sub-group of outcasts from that culture. The pains of the unemployment process depicted here are very much about the failure to fulfill the conventional requirements of a real man: success, defiance, and a mask of invulnerability. . . . [Ultimately] unforeseen changes allow these outcasts to return to the comfort and reassurance of the traditional mainstream culture, improved by their chastening and instructive brush with the resurgence of an unemployment subculture, but allowed by good fortune to rejoin respectable macho society. (2011)

Political scientist Bruce Baum adds, "*The Company Men* . . . personifies the contrast between good and bad capitalism. It brings to life the high human costs of the recession that resulted from the financial crisis . . . [showing] how contemporary capitalism has gone awry, particularly in the United States, without suggesting that capitalism is unredeemable" (2011, 608). That is why, Baum continues, "Bobby is not thoroughly heartless and amoral. [H]e may have been hooked by the perks of bad capitalism but his underlying decency ultimately finds expression, and he becomes, with Gene, an agent of a storybook good capitalism" (609).

In a sense, then, *The Company Men* is a film version of a bad economy happening to good people. As the tagline for the film conveys, "In America, we give our lives to our jobs. It's time to take them back." This "taking back" can be read as a reclaiming of white male Americanness in the face of a threat to this quintessential representation of American citizenship. It is within this reclamation that, according to the familiar narrative, white American masculinity can be recovered and even redeemed. In turn, this redemption casts away threat and shores up the security of white masculinity—with America itself being reconstituted through these characters.

LARRY CROWNE:
SCOOTING THROUGH THE GREAT RECESSION

Similar to *The Company Men*, *Larry Crowne* begins with the main character going to work in the morning. Different from Bobby's glamorous job, however, Larry (Tom Hanks) works at U-Mart, a fictional discount chain store. Also in contrast with Bobby's initial arrogance, Larry is humble from the start and seems to take infinite pride in the job he does. Yet, like Bobby, Larry is fired from his job within the first few minutes of the film. The most important difference between these two films is the fact that *The Company Men* positions Bobby's firing within the context of recession, whereas Larry's firing occurs without much context, other than Larry being told that he is being let go because he does not have college experience. In fact, the entire movie goes out of its way to avoid the Great Recession and maintains the illusion that Larry is simply starting a new life. The insensitive implication here is that, as Hanks conveys in the interview quoted from earlier, being fired was "the best thing to ever happen to Larry."

Although *Larry Crowne* is the most subtle of the films discussed in this chapter in engaging and portraying the Great Recession, the film does offer viewers glimpses of it. By so doing, the film is clearly positioned within this specific time period. For instance, Larry conveys on a couple of occasions, "Times are tough." He buys a scooter from his neighbor because his SUV proves too expensive to keep filled. One of his former bosses at U-Mart is also fired and ends up delivering pizza. And perhaps most indicative of the time period in question is that Larry enacts a "strategic foreclosure" on his house—a new phenomenon of the Great Recession—

taking all paperwork and keys to the bank. Larry then rents a tiny apartment, which also speaks to the thousands of Americans who had to downsize during this time.

However, as Marshall Fine reflects in a piece for the *Huffington Post*:

> The conflict is minimal; so, seemingly, is the stress of unem-
> ployment on Larry (though he does take a job, working in a
> Navy buddy's restaurant as a short-order cook). This approach
> seems counter-intuitive, at a time when the nerve-wracking day-
> to-day reality for many people is job insecurity, foreclosure and
> loss, the continuing ripple effect of Bush-era economics. (2011)

Because of this portrayal of the Great Recession, Peter Travers, writing for *Rolling Stone*, calls *Larry Crowne* "alarmingly, depressingly out of touch" (2011). Namely, this is a film situated within the Great Recession, that should address the recession, given its topic, but that turns on being disconnected from this very topic and context. In his review for the *New York Times*, Stephen Holden offers a similar take:

> The film [rapidly loses] interest in the devastating impact of the
> unemployment crisis on the middle class. After addressing the
> excruciating financial particulars of Larry's situation, the movie
> concentrates on his college education. While a student, he con-
> veniently lands a new job as a cook in a coffee shop. Having
> barely paid lip service to today's hard economic realities, the
> movie abandons any pretense of relevance and gets to the cutesy
> stuff. (2011)

It is the cutesy stuff that makes the film most out of touch and disengaged. After being fired, Larry enrolls in community college where he excels in his classes, falls in love, and ends up with one of his professors, Mercedes (Julia Roberts). He hangs out with a scooter gang of twenty-something-year-olds, who give him and his house makeovers on a dime. Even if it goes unstated, it is clear that

Larry's biggest threat is the economy, which he tackles with a can-do attitude and smile. In the end, Larry is redeemed from having lost his job and house, as he "gets the girl." Perhaps more importantly, he does not seem affected in any negative way by his losses. This could very well be the biggest win for white masculinity reinforced within this film.

Because of the scooter gang, some of his classmates, and his neighbors (who are black), *Larry Crowne* is the most multiethnic and multiracial of the films analyzed in this chapter. However, like the others, this film is about a middle-aged white American man, Larry, who is starting over. The fact that he, different from so many people in real life, has the resources to begin anew is never questioned or explained. After all, his resources are somewhat limited, since he had to surrender his house. But he is nonetheless able to attend college, and a friend hires him as a cook—possibilities, we might assume, related to his military background. It is Larry's black neighbor, Lamar (Cedric the Entertainer), who fittingly describes Larry's life when he tells him that he has his health and pale skin. These will help Larry to start over with a clean slate. This is likely the best lesson that *Larry Crowne* has to offer.

Again, this film underscores the burden on white men in times of crisis, and it does so in a way that redeems them. Within *Larry Crowne*, the burden actually appears negligible with its rehearsal of narratives around individualism, hard work, and optimism. That is, even in the face of loss, white American men should remember that they can find goodness and redemption, and even when the bottom has dropped out and others are reeling from devastation, mainstream Americans should remember to remain hopeful. This message is conveyed to American viewers in a decade book-ended by traumatic events: September 11, 2001, on the one end, and the Great Recession, on the other.

UP IN THE AIR: THE (UN)GROUNDEDNESS OF
MIDDLE-AGED WHITE MEN

As discussed earlier, Reitman was one of the more vocal directors in his assertion that he did not intend to make a recession film. He states, "I thought I was making a movie about a single man, about a guy who was trying to figure out who and what he wanted in his life. [O]ver the course of writing it, the world changed. So the film just began to reflect what was going on" (*Oprah Magazine* 2010). As with any film, however, *Up in the Air* does more than *reflect* what is happening; rather, it presents viewers with an understanding of circumstances. In this case, the situation is that of a middle-aged white man, Ryan Bingham (George Clooney), as a "transition specialist"; he fires people, he says, when "bosses do not have the balls to fire their employees." The Great Recession has provided him with a steady income. In fact, Ryan protects himself from threats of life by traveling 352 days of the year—making the airport and airplane "home." In his words, "All the things you probably hate about travelling—the recycled air, the artificial lighting, the digital juice dispensers, the cheap sushi, are warm reminders that I'm home." Perhaps more importantly, the airport and airplane have become Ryan's identity. He conveys, "To know me is to fly with me." Thus, this ungroundedness represents life itself. As Ryan succinctly tells attendees of his motivational lecture, "Moving is living."

In an interview with PopSugar Entertainment, Reitman characterizes Ryan Bingham as an antihero. He explains:

> I don't know why I'm drawn to anti-heroes but I certainly am. [H]umanizing good people is kind of boring and I don't really see the value in it. Showing romance of two people who are just kind of charming and deserve each other, what's the work in that, what's the value in that? Humanizing tricky characters for me is exhilarating and making audience films out of indie sub-

jects excites me. At the end of the day I don't know why I'm drawn to it. (2009)

Ryan is certainly the film's main character, and he is presented as someone with whom viewers can feel comfortable and for whom they can root. In his analysis of the film, Edward Mitchell maintains that *Up in the Air*

> circles broad cultural issues, pitting Ryan Bingham against the backdrop of economic recession. Bingham, a self-proclaimed "mutation, a new species," a "spaceman" with immaterial goals, moves through the "margins of itineraries"—airports, hotels, and conference rooms—making " fast friends," floating unencumbered by the baggage that anchors his more terrestrial relations. (2012, 9–10)

Mitchell concludes, "Bingham is simply a soft landing for the inevitable crash—a twinkle-eyed fantasy that will fade into dusk" (2012, 11). Ryan's fantasy does come crashing after he falls for Alex Goran (Vera Farmiga), another "ungrounded" fellow traveler he meets in his travels. In his connection with Alex, Ryan begins not to mind "baggage" for the first time. He even walks out of a lecture in which he is supposed to tell attendees that baggage holds them back.

Thus, the growth that antihero Ryan Bingham experiences is in relation to his personal connections and not to what he does for a living. In fact, it seems as though firing people takes no emotional toll on him at all. After all, he has a *system* for "letting people go"—one that remains consistent throughout the film. Ryan appears completely untouched by the world around him. While going through the Detroit airport with coworker Natalie Keener (Anna Kendrick), for instance, they walk past a group of uniformed soldiers on their way to deployments. Neither character pays any attention to the soldiers. Nevertheless, Ryan is somewhat affected by the slow economy when Natalie, freshly out of college, develops an innovative way for him and his coworkers to do their jobs through computers. This would mean avoiding all travel—threatening not only Ryan's livelihood but also his lifestyle and his very identity. In the end, the film leaves Ryan's personal and work life "up in the air." He discovers that Alex is married and has a family. With this, he no longer feels quite the same about traveling. However, it is clear to viewers that the antihero will survive the struggling economy, even if he might emerge changed and even somewhat damaged. In general, then, this is a story about resilience for the main character. In viewing the recession through this character's eyes, American viewers are comforted that they too can survive. Significantly, Ryan's survival is accomplished through a refusal to ground himself, and in this sense, he averts danger more than he confronts it. This averting of danger likewise connects to the way that *Larry Crowne* avoids the topic of recession, thereby offering viewers a more upbeat and less traumatic story.

WALL STREET: MONEY NEVER SLEEPS: GORDON GEKKO AS THE QUINTESSENTIAL 9/11 WHITE MAN

Wall Street: Money Never Sleeps begins with Gordon Gekko (Michael Douglas) being released from prison in 2001. As Gordon steps out, no one is there to greet him or to take him home, and his aloneness is evident. The film fast-forwards to 2008, where Gordon is now a published author and his estranged daughter, Winnie (Carey Mulligan), is remaking her life with her boyfriend, Jake Moore (Shia LaBeouf), a Wall Street trader. In the dynamic between Gordon and Jake, Gordon represents old, cynical greed, while Jake offers viewers a new breed of Wall Street broker and trader—one seemingly invested not only in money but also in the future. Jake shows loyalty to the institution by being overcome by the death of his boss, Lou Zebel (Frank Langella), who commits suicide after his firm goes bankrupt.

The film develops within a context of fast-paced change that begins with the release of Gordon a little more than a month after the September 11, 2001, attacks. As viewers see, the date is October 21, 2001. A shot of the headline from a newspaper still covers the events, featuring the words "Ground Zero." Viewers receive another historical cue just prior to Lou's suicide in 2008, when they see a headline from the *New York Post* and a picture of Barack Obama with the caption "Destiny," referring to his presidential nomination. These headlines create a chronology of sorts and position the film within a specific moment—that highlighted by the present project itself—with the events of September 11, 2001, and those of September 16, 2008, providing its perimeter.

Other signifiers help to position *Wall Street: Money Never Sleeps* within a 9/11 context and situate its tropes within the *9/11 project*. For instance, at one point Gordon gives a talk in a lecture hall and remarks that trillions of dollars of credit are "WMDs, weapons of mass destruction"—a concept with which his audience and viewers of the film are quite acquainted. Another example occurs when Winnie talks with her dad for the first time in years, during a truncated dinner, and remarks that her online publication has gained a steady readership since their coverage of "Mission Accomplished"—a reference to President Bush's premature Iraq victory statement aboard the USS *Abraham Lincoln* in 2003. These signifiers serve two functions: They help viewers to place the film in a 9/11 historical context, and they provide viewers with familiar ways of marking and understanding the plot. Along with over a dozen references to "bubbles," both real and metaphorical, these markers allow those watching the film to identify with the familiar sensibilities of the time period (for example, housing and financial bubbles). This is why the economic collapse is described in the film as the end of the world—a description comparable to that used to describe the events of September 11, 2001, and an idea to which we return in our final chapter on 9/11 apocalyptic films.

Within the film, Gordon's character interests us the most, as he simultaneously embodies a recent past, the present, and the future. Reviewing the film for the *New Statesman*, Ryan Gilbey conveys, "If the defining flaw of the first *Wall Street* film was its refusal to cut its ties with Gekko, then the sequel suffers from a similar excess of fidelity to the character" (2010). Toward the end of the film, after he has dispossessed Winnie and Jake of one hundred million dollars, most of which he had given to Winnie before he went to prison, Gordon tells Jake, "It's not about the money, it's about the game." After his heist, Gordon reinvents himself, although unimaginatively, for he becomes a person similar to the one he was before incarceration. Or, perhaps, viewers are to think that a decade in prison has had no effect on him. At one point, he calls someone and says to whoever answers the phone to tell them, "Gordon Gekko is back." Jake even offers him a relationship with his as-yet unborn grandchild if he returns the principal of the money he stole from Winnie, to which Gordon responds, "That's a trade I cannot make." Gordon does show up at the end of the film but not to ask for forgiveness. Rather, he seeks to justify his actions to his daughter.

The economy presents both an opportunity and a threat to Gordon. That is, after paying for his earlier greed with a decade of imprisonment, he becomes a reinvented version of himself (even if he has retained certain flaws). Gordon appears to believe that the behaviors leading to his incarceration are now part and parcel of the Wall Street operation. The most telling of his ideas comes as a flippant pronouncement about greed made in the same lecture in which he references WMDs. He states, "Now seems it's legal." Gordon eventually convinces Winnie to give him (and Jake) a second chance by arguing that all human beings are "mixed bags." In a review for the *New York Times*, A. O. Scott maintains, "To the question, 'What went wrong?' the film offers an answer that is both irrefutable and unsatisfying: human nature" (2011).

Most clearly situated at the intersection of September 11, 2001, and the Great Recession, *Wall Street: Money Never Sleeps* offers a historical lesson around trauma and resilience. Gordon is presented as a character always "landing on his feet," even in the wake of an unprecedented landscape. This is a character capable of remaking himself, negotiating new territory, and emerging strong. Significantly, the character's older age serves to address vulnerabilities around aging as it relates to whiteness and masculinity (recall suicides of other older characters addressed in this chapter). In turn, and by extension, American viewers can feel that their country will positively emerge from threatening and precarious times. In all four films addressed, defeat is not an option—neither for white American men nor for the United States of America.

CONCLUSION

In a *New York Times* article, Annie Lowrey discusses a 2013 study by the Urban Institute showing that although "millions of Americans suffered a loss of wealth during the recession and the sluggish recovery that followed, the last half a decade has proved far worse for black and Hispanic families than for white families" (2013). In a different column, also for the *New York Times*, and using data from the U.S. Census Bureau to compare hours worked by age in 2007 (one year before the recession) and 2010 (two years after the recession), economics professor Casey Mulligan shows that people between the ages of sixteen and twenty-six were hardest hit by the economic downturn. Hollywood, however, has been intent to tell a different story—that of middle- and upper-middle-class, middle-aged, white men and their experiences with the Great Recession. Overall, the central characters we discuss are portrayed as making their way through economic threat—a threat that directly or indirectly undermines their livelihoods and identities. Central to these stories, but also unspoken, is their white masculinity.

In closing, we can briefly raise an additional theme that unites these four films and that also links them back to previous films discussed in this project: that of "home." We can begin with a literal interpretation with Bobby (*The Company Men*) and Larry (*Larry Crowne*), who lose their houses to unemployment. However, this literal conception of home is accompanied by a more metaphorical one, as both men are initially rather lost and without purpose. They slowly work to find their way home, meaning their way to security within a changing world. For Bobby, this process is quite painful, while for Larry, it is less distressing. For both characters, viewers see depictions of displacement and the need to manage unfamiliar terrain. All of the main male characters, in fact, lose their familiar landscape. In response, they struggle, to varying degrees, to (re)gain this lost security.

Wall Street: Money Never Sleeps and *Up in the Air* present the theme of home fairly straightforwardly. In fact, songs with lyrics about home frame both films. In *Wall Street: Money Never Sleeps*, the David Byrne song, "Home," conveys the following lines: "I'm looking for a home, where the wheels are turning. Home, why I keep returning."

Similarly, midway through *Up in the Air*, when Ryan and Natalie are in the midst of firing people across the country, viewers see Ryan walking into companies and through airports. The Dan Auerbach song "Goin' Home" plays in the background: "I've spent too long away from home. . . . So long, I'm goin', goin' home."

Thus we are to consider these characters as representing a sort of transience and impermanence vis-à-vis home. These notions recall anxiety over the fast-paced and changing world, discussed in chapter 4 with respect to 9/11 monsters. In a 9/11 world, it is the threat of this change—the sudden and "out of the blue" quality—that brings together the events of September 11, 2001, and those of September 16, 2008. Various means of coping and managing this altered landscape inform these and other 9/11 Hollywood films, as well as the general feeling of displacement and loss framing our most recent decade.

Chapter Eight

9/11 End-of-Days Hollywood

At some point, we may be the only ones left. That's OK with me. We are America—President G.W. Bush. (Woodward and Balz 2002)

In October 2005 a CNN/*USA Today*/Gallup poll showed that 62 percent of Americans thought it was very or somewhat likely that the avian flu would strike the United States, and 52 percent were very or somewhat confident that the federal government could handle an epidemic (Saad 2005). In the same poll, only 24 percent of respondents were worried that either they or someone in their family would be a victim of the avian flu virus (Saad 2005). Almost a month later, Gallup asked Americans "to name the most urgent health problem facing the country at the present time," and 10 percent named the avian flu. The previous year, only 2 percent had named the avian flu as an urgent problem, showing an eight-point increase and the highest percentage ever recorded by Gallup in response to this question (Carroll 2005). Moreover, 50 percent of Americans expressed being very or somewhat worried about experiencing "a deadly virus such as bird flu or something similar, that spreads to the United States from a foreign country," and 43 percent expressed being very or somewhat worried about experiencing "a deadly infectious disease such as smallpox or something similar, that is brought into the United States by terrorists" (Carroll 2005).

To put these numbers in perspective, 2005 did experience a major outbreak of the avian flu, although a total of 125 people had been infected in several Asian countries at the time of this polling and about half of these people had died (CNN.com 2005). From 2003 to 2013, 649 cases were identified worldwide, and 385 people died during this decade. The closest reported case was in Canada, with the remaining cases being in the Middle East, Asia, or Africa. Indonesia reported the highest number of cases and deaths—195 and 163 respectively (CNN.com 2014). These poll numbers demonstrate two important elements of the *9/11 project* addressed in this chapter: (1) anxiety among Americans—this time manifest as fear of a major, catastrophic, and contagious illness within the United States; and (2) an overreliance on the government to manage such an event. The films analyzed below project both of these elements.

Hollywood enactments of stories involving the end of the world, and/or of menacing monsters and the undead, are not new. Film scholars have argued that social anxiety about economic or political uncertainty at various points in history has traditionally given rise to a number of films with apocalyptic under- and overtones. Speaking of the time period encompassed by the 1940s to 1950s, Ruby Rich underscores the relationship between text and context: "The science fiction and monster films [during those decades] . . . can be used to link representational styles and narrative tropes to specific political and scientific hysterias" of that time (2004). As an example, the original *War of the Worlds* (Byron Haskin, 1953), a film about aliens attacking Earth, came out in the midst of the Cold War and fears of a Communist invasion. The point, of course, can be expanded to any decade or time period. The original *Dracula* (Tod Browning and Karl Freund, 1931) was released during the Great Depression, when anxieties about the economy were understandably heightened. Also the product of the Cold War era, *The Day After* (Nicholas Meyer, 1983) depicted a horrendous nuclear holocaust as experienced by people in the U.S. Midwest. It is therefore no surprise that specific political, social, and scientific hysterias culminate in representations of the apocalypse or what Richard Walsh dubs "the mother of all catastrophes, the world's tragic finale" (2010).

Falling in line with this history, the twenty-first century has witnessed an out-of-the-ordinary increase in (post-)apocalyptic films of various genres. In the words of John Walliss and James Aston, "There has . . . been a significant increase in apocalyptic imagery and themes post-9/11 across a variety of popular media" and " the most popular medium for conveying the apocalypse has been cinema" (2011, 54). In fact, since the events of September 11, 2001, Hollywood has become a prolific purveyor of films (and hence themes) about global pandemics, altered world orders, and the overall impending end of the world, in which comedies, dramas, action films, and even animated films for children all offer end-of-the-world scenarios. Thus, and following Douglas Kellner's point that "Hollywood films provide important cinematic visions concerning the psychological, sociopolitical, and ideological make-up of U.S. society at a given point in history" (2011, 18), in this conclusion, we seek to apply the discussion developed in previous chapters about race, gender, and nation, to explore the psychological, sociopolitical, and ideological components of 9/11 apocalyptic films. We argue that, exacerbated by official governmental rhetoric, the specific anxieties generated by the September 11, 2001, events have made apocalyptic films a common occurrence at this particular historical juncture. To illustrate, there were fifty-nine apocalyptic films released in the twenty-year span between 1980 and 1999, whereas there were close to ninety released in the thirteen-year span between 2001 and 2013 (Anonymous 2013).

Kellner conveys, "Cinematic wars over issues like terrorism, war and militarism, the environment, rights, and other issues have been intensely fought in the 2000s on the terrain of Hollywood cinema" (2011, 3). We have shown in earlier chapters how some of these "wars" involving representations of terrorism, militarism, race, gender, and the economy have unfolded in particular films. Here, we would like to expand our analytical frame to consider how Hollywood has channeled certain 9/11 anxieties and ideologies into apocalyptic film projects. In an interview with Jordan Hoffman, *Contagion* (2011) director Steven Soderbergh compares 9/11 anxieties reflected in recent films with PTSD. In his words:

> There's no question that the country still hasn't processed what happened ten years ago and we're still in some form of post-traumatic stress syndrome. Whether or not this is a manifestation of that, I don't know. I mean, this kind of fantasy, or contemplation may be a better word, is something that movies do really well. They always have. (Hoffman 2011)

While we agree that contemplating apocalyptic scenarios is something that (Hollywood) films do well, we would argue that it has been something that they have done supremely well after September 11, 2001.

As we have maintained in this project and elsewhere, although the events of September 11, 2001, themselves triggered certain anxieties among the public, these anxieties were heightened by an official governmental rhetoric that created an "us and them" dynamic that reactivated old ideologies and created new ones (Bloodsworth-Lugo and Lugo-Lugo 2010). It is important to note that although Hollywood, at times, contests the official rhetoric by providing viewers with alternative points of view, it has often fallen in line with it, merely recreating the anxieties embedded within the official narrative. In this regard, we agree with David Holloway, who argues, "If Hollywood appeared to be politicized after 9/11, this was often because the Bush administration's response helped heighten existing trends . . . not because the 9/11 attacks functioned as a moment of radical epiphany that changed the face of mainstream Hollywood film (2008, 82). As such, the rhetoric developed by the Bush administration served as a modulator of ideas, including ideas about the global reach of terrorism and the changing of the United States (as in "the day that changed America forever") and the world. President Bush stated on September 20, 2001, regarding the global reach of terrorism, "This is not . . . just America's fight. And what is at stake is not just America's freedom. This is the world's fight" (Bush 2001). The perception that terrorism and the fight against it is now a global phenomenon has been one of the ideas informing 9/11 apocalyptic films.

Moreover, President Bush stated in his 2002 State of the Union speech, "This time of adversity offers a unique moment of opportunity—a moment we must seize to change our culture. . . . And we have a great opportunity during this time of war to lead the world toward the values that will bring lasting peace" (2002a). The idea that massive change must occur or has occurred is also present in the following remark from 2004: "After 9-11, the world changed for me, and I think changed for the country . . . because . . . we assumed oceans would protect us from harm. And that's not the case. It's not the reality of the 21st century" (Bush 2004). Ideas about impending or necessary cultural and global change have also been at the center of Hollywood 9/11 end-of-the-world scenarios. In our view, these ideas have been informed by 9/11 ideologies involving terrorism, insecurity, and change.

Marc Redfield claims, "There has never been a more utterly mediated event" than September 11, 2001 (2009, 26), declaring that the name-date we know as "September 11" or "9/11" very quickly " became a slogan . . . around which nationalist energies could be marshaled" and for which "the language of war—of a putatively new kind of absolute war, a 'war on terror'—so definitely closed down other possibilities for official response" (1). This idea of an "absolute war" has informed dimensions of 9/11 apocalyptic films. The absolute war began with the apocalyptic images of the collapsing Twin Towers projected onto our television screens, repeatedly, on September 11, 2001. Discussing these images, Redfield states that what unfolded on television "seemed akin to a particular cinematic genre: the big-budget disaster movie" (2009, 27). Melnick complements Redfield's assessment, referring to the television portrayals of the event as a " telethon," and contending that discussions of popular culture violence after September 11, 2001, were fed "by the notion that the mode of attack was somehow inextricable from visual codes developed by Hollywood" (2009, 50). Redfield cites director Robert Altman who, a month after the events, declared, "Nobody would have thought to commit an atrocity like that unless they'd seen it in a movie" (50).

The images shown on television contributed to the creation of a specific rhetoric and sensibility, which in turn, affected the creation of Hollywood narratives. Holloway offers insight into the power that 9/11 rhetoric and discourse had on the public:

> If one thing was clear after 9/11, it was the continued appeal to versions of American nationalism that were aggressively affirmative of existing American institutions and political/economic structures—an appeal that was particularly powerful . . . because it was embraced almost as widely by Americans who dissented from the hegemonic narrative, as by those who signed up to it. (2008, 158)

Although we agree with Redfield and Melnick's assessments of the disaster-movie quality of both the images and narrative around the events of September 11, 2001, and the effects of these images on the collective American psyche, we will focus on a somewhat different angle here. That is, we highlight the influence of the rhetoric around the events on actual disaster movies produced after September 11, 2001, especially disaster movies that are decidedly apocalyptic. To that effect, we analyze three recently released films: *Take Shelter* (2011), *Contagion*, and *World War Z* (2013). We offer these films as illustrations of the main arguments addressed throughout the book involving the *9/11 project*, its sensibilities, and its attendant ideologies.

TAKE SHELTER: THE END IS NEAR AND ANXIETY AS THE APOCALYPSE

Take Shelter is the most psychologically heavy of the three films discussed in this chapter and perhaps the entire book. The film uses Curtis LaForche (Michael Shannon), a working-class husband and father, to blur the lines between social and psychological anxieties, as he experiences visions and nightmares about an impending, catastrophic storm. Viewers see Curtis consumed with the anxiety produced by these visions and nightmares, desperately trying to build a shelter for his family before the big event. The film is set in a small blue-collar town in Ohio, giving a "middle of America" feel to the action. That Curtis's wife, Samantha (Jessica Chastain), is a stay-at-home mom, and his daughter, Hannah (Tova Stewart), is deaf, contribute to the feel of these characters as "everyday people." The nature and meaning of Curtis's psychological episodes get complicated for viewers when they learn that Curtis's mother developed schizophrenia when she was approximately his age. This complication gives *Take Shelter* its significance, for viewers are never quite certain whether Curtis's anxieties, including his hallucinations and nightmares, are the result of a sort of visionary clarity or a genetic condition enveloping the mind of a father and husband who is ultimately trying to protect his family. This contention is never resolved, for the ending is as ambiguous as the rest of the film in this respect, although viewers are led to think that psychological anxieties can have catastrophic consequences for everyone.

Viewers watch Curtis drop everything in his life, including his job, friends, and community, to build an underground shelter on his property. At times he transforms into a modern-day Noah, warning people about the impending major flood. He tells his neighbors, "You think I'm crazy? Well, listen up, there's a storm coming like nothing you've ever seen, and not a one of you is prepared for it." Later he tells them, "Sleep well in your beds. 'Cause if this thing comes true, there ain't gonna be any more." Gareth Higgins, in his article for *Sojourners* magazine, describes *Take Shelter* as "a powerful portrayal of individual trauma and communal ignorance that takes very seriously the conventional—and counterproductive—response to recent global uncertainty" (2012). "Conventional," because of its individualistic approach, and "counterproductive," because the blurred lines between social and psychological anxieties and mental illness justify communal ignorance. Viewers see that a storm does come through the town, and although it causes some damage, it is not the kind that Curtis had envisioned or described. He takes his family to the shelter he had built, where they stay until the storm passes.

Writing for the *New York Times*, A. O. Scott provides, perhaps, the most interesting and 9/11-like description of *Take Shelter*. In his words:

The greatest fear a man can experience is that of losing the good life he has. It is this anxiety, which afflicts Curtis in an especially virulent form, that defines the mood of *Take Shelter*. It is a quiet, relentless exploration of the latent (and not so latent) terrors that bedevil contemporary American life, a horror movie that will trouble your sleep not with visions of monsters but with a more familiar dread. We like to think that individually and collectively, we have it pretty good, but it is harder and harder to allay the suspicion that a looming disaster—economic or environmental, human or divine—might come along and destroy it all. Normalcy can feel awfully precarious, like a comforting dream blotting out a nightmarish reality. (2011)

The power of *Take Shelter* lies precisely in its ability to convey this sense of dread, using the big storm as an all-encompassing metaphor whereby "vast oceans can no longer protect us." The film evokes "enemies lurking in shadows," unimaginable tragedy, and an all-encompassing uncertainty—all within Small Town, U.S.A.

CONTAGION: 9/11 ANXIETY AROUND DWINDLING NUMBERS

Released on the tenth anniversary of the September 11, 2001, events (almost to the day), and positioned within 9/11 ideologies and institutions, the plot of *Contagion* takes viewers to the rapid spread of a disease no one has witnessed and that scientists name Mer-1. The film begins on day two of the spreading disease, when Beth Emhoff (Gwyneth Paltrow) becomes sick, after returning to Minneapolis from a trip to Hong Kong, with a layover in Chicago. Viewers glimpse an individual in Hong Kong and another in London who seem to share the same symptoms. As viewers receive images and indications of the disease, they are also shown the number of inhabitants in major cities around the world: Hong Kong, 2.1 million people; London, 8.6 million people; Minneapolis, 3.6 million people; and Tokyo, 36.8 million people. These are the first indications viewers receive about the potential global impacts that a disease such as this could have, given that a person could be in Hong Kong one day and Minneapolis the next, infecting hundreds or thousands of people in between.

Beth and her son, Clark (Griffin Kane), die the following day. While explaining the situation to Beth's husband, Mitch Emhoff (Matt Damon), the doctor matter-of-factly states, "Some people get a disease and live, some get sicker and die," suggesting that even experts are sometimes wrong. After an autopsy is performed on Beth's body, the Center for Disease Control (CDC) is called and Epidemic Intelligence Officer Dr. Erin Mears (Kate Winslet) is sent

to Minneapolis to investigate. An on-site team and the CDC begin
monitoring and tracking the spread of the disease, as there appear to
be thirty-two confirmed cases and five deaths at this point. Ten
days later there are over eight million people infected by the virus.
It is Dr. Mears who provides the tagline for the film, when she says
to one of Beth's coworkers, who has also gotten sick after picking
Beth up at the airport: "Don't talk to anyone, don't touch anyone.
That's the most important thing." Her words provide a second clue
as to the global impacts of such a disease, since not talking to
anyone or touching anyone become impossibilities in a large city
and for people who travel by mass transit and airplane on a daily or
regular basis (Beth's coworker was on a public bus when Mears
gives him the directive).

The global proportions of the pandemic are highlighted by the
fact that the World Health Organization sends an epidemiologist,
Dr. Leonora Orantes (Marion Cotillard), to Hong Kong to investigate the origins of the disease. While Dr. Orantes is trying to determine the origin, she ends up being abducted as collateral in an
effort by members of a village to ensure that all village residents
get vaccinated. In this Hollywood incarnation of "the end is near,"
residents of nations in the global South are aware that not all of
those infected are treated equally. In the end, the effort backfires on
members of the village, as they are given placebos in exchange for
the doctor's return. This serves as commentary that the lives of
people residing in the global South are indeed not as important as
the life of one doctor from the global North. Not only does the
doctor get rescued, she is also immediately offered the vaccine.

The film is replete with allusions to 9/11 rhetoric and ideologies.
These begin from the moment the CDC becomes involved in the
process, as agents and military personnel from the Homeland Security Administration (HSA)—the quintessential 9/11 governmental institution—take charge of the course, tone, and tenor of the
investigation. The first thing the HSA and military personnel do is

debrief Dr. Ellis Cheever (Laurence Fishburn) about the disease, asking him whether there is a chance that it could have been weaponized. What they primarily want to know is whether terrorists could have weaponized the bird flu, to which Dr. Cheever responds, "Someone doesn't have to weaponize the bird flu. The birds are doing that." In his review for *The New Yorker*, David Denby offers that *Contagion* "could become an event in an ongoing political debate over the nature of American life." He remarks:

> *Contagion* is, of course, a 9/11-anniversary movie, though probably not one that the public was expecting. Soderbergh appears to be saying, "I'll show you something far worse than a terrorist attack, and no fundamentalist fanatic planned it." The film suggests that, at any moment, our advanced civilization could be close to a breakdown exacerbated by precisely what is most advanced in it. And the movie shows us something else: heroic work by scientists and Homeland Security officials. We can't help noticing that with two exceptions . . . the heroes are all employees of the federal government, and instinctively factual people. (2011)

Joshua Clover offers a useful critique of Soderbergh's overinvestment in governmental figures. In his words, "What is so retrograde about the film, finally, is the quiet persistence with which it solicits the audience's sympathies for the authorities. In a world gone catastrophically wrong, the only folks to be trusted are government officials, mostly aligned with the Center for Disease Control" (2011). We view this depiction as a direct reflection of 9/11, when Americans looked for answers and comfort in the words and actions of President Bush and his administration in the wake of the September 11, 2001, events.

The film also presents the quick militarization of the U.S. landscape, as soldiers are deployed across the country to monitor and close the borders of various cities/states, creating checkpoints similar to the ones seen in portrayals of the United States–Mexico border or Israel. The film shows a further 9/11-ification of the pandemic in the language utilized. For instance, when explaining the situation at a press conference, Dr. Cheever says, "The first job with these things is always to find ground zero." Given the feeling of emergency and urgency conveyed by the film, the reference to "ground zero" unequivocally transports viewers back to September 11, 2001, and creates a sense of continuity between real events and fictional ones in the film. Perhaps more importantly, it provides viewers with a lens through which to view and interpret the film's events.

As the film progresses and people stay at home to avoid contact with other people, viewers see shots of empty public places such as gyms, malls, and more tellingly, airports—another poignant reference to September 11, 2001. The film incorporates and presents a veiled critique of the conspiracy theories stemming from, and fomenting panic and anxiety after, the events of September 11, 2001, in a character named Alan Krumwiede (Jude Law), a fringe journalist intent on proving that the disease is a conspiracy by the government. Krumwiede maintains that the government knows of a cheap cure already available; he mentions "forsythia" as this known cure and makes an online video in which he claims to be sick and taking the remedy. Before the vaccine is available, Dr. Cheever offers a television interview to rebut the journalist's claims, stating:

> We're working very hard to find out where this virus came from. To treat it and to vaccinate against it if we can. We don't know all of that yet, we just don't know. What we do know is that in order to become sick you have to first come in contact with a sick person or something that they touched. In order to get scared, all you have to do is to come in contact with a rumor, or the television, or the Internet. I think what Mr. Krumwiede is uh . . . is spreading, is far more dangerous than the disease.

The implication, of course, is that Krumwiede is spreading fear, ignorance, and mistrust in the government, all of which can wreak havoc on an already fragile society. The inclusion of a strong conspiracy theory element in the plot, even though viewers learn that Krumwiede is acting in bad faith as he never had the virus and is actually looking for financial gain, is important, for as Arthur Goldwag suggests, conspiracy theories are a way for those who feel impotent over events and circumstances to articulate an explanation (2009). The way that Krumwiede pushes for information is reminiscent of the way certain groups pressed for answers after the events of September 11, 2001, suggesting government involvement in those events.

WORLD WAR Z: THE ZOMBIE APOCALYPSE AND ANXIETIES ABOUT THE "OTHER"

Films about zombies and/or monsters are not new. New are the *global* representations of zombies and monsters, implicating new forms of technology into the zombie-fication or monster-fication of the world. Levina and Bui argue that the rapidly changing world of the twenty-first century has fostered specific fears and tensions that reflect "an interconnected global environment where increased mobility of people, technologies, and disease have produced great social, political, and economic uncertainty" (2013, 1). They conclude by reasoning that "over the past decade, we have been terrorized by change" (1). In an interview with Lucien Flores for the *Daily Free Press*, director Marc Forster candidly states, "We're living in a time of change and I think every time the world's been through such a transformation, zombies have been very, very popular" (2013).

It is no coincidence, then, as we discussed earlier, that 9/11 films about monsters—including zombies—have acquired a global focus. This brings us back to the words of President Bush that terrorism is "the world's fight." Nicole Birch-Bayley suggests that 9/11 zombie films have become explicitly concerned "with a crisis culture" (2012). She suggests that in a shift of the global media after the September 11, 2001, attacks, "zombie films came to reflect the worst-case fears of an apprehensive media culture, entertaining the same anxieties about world events, in this case, a fear of terrorism and epidemic in the zombie form" (2012, 1137). Talking to Jamie Lincoln for *Interview* magazine, director Marc Forster argues:

> I think people, unfortunately, live in constant fear. I think the government—and people in general—create scenarios people fear, because ultimately through fear you can control people. I wish we could live in a world where there would be no fear, but it's a driving force in many decisions people make these days, whether it's personal, economic, or even job-related. (Lincoln 2013)

Anxieties and fears about terrorism have given 9/11 zombie films their trademark, which is to say, their global scope. Different from films such as *The Dawn of the Dead* (George A. Ramero, 1979), which takes place in a shopping mall in Philadelphia with an implication that, perhaps, the rest of the world has also become zombie-fied, 9/11 zombie films such as *28 Days Later* (Danny Boyle, 2003), present the zombie-fication of the population as an actual global phenomenon—a challenge that individuals in the global North must contend with and fight in order to survive.

World War Z presents viewers with interesting ideological reversals on the security/threat narrative. Different from other zombie representations, the zombies in *World War Z* are fast (very fast) and unpredictable, posing a clear and rapid danger to humans. The speed of the zombies establishes the pace for the narrative, building and projecting a sense of urgency. David Denby conveys that the film "evokes the hectic density of modern life; it stirs fears of plague and anarchy, and the feeling that everything is constantly accelerating. At times, it has the tone and the tempo of panic"

(2013). At one point in the film, when the main character is being briefed about the scope of the "plague," viewers see a screen with a running tally similar to the costofwar.com website by the National Priorities Program—the website used to track the cost of the wars in Iraq and Afghanistan. The running tally seen in the film is of human beings infected and transformed into zombies. The precipitous climbing of the numbers on the screen represents the rapid loss of humanity by this inexplicable event. This is compounded by the loss of sociopolitical structure, for as different from *Contagion*, we learn very early in *World War Z*, that most (if not all) members of the U.S. government are gone. In fact, the United Nations is now in charge.

The government is not the only thing gone in the world of *World War Z*. From the very beginning, viewers understand that for the characters in the film there is no home. All they have left is their humanity—and each other. This is made explicit, when once secured in a United Nations command ship, Karin Lane (Mirelle Enos) changes the name of her satellite phone from "Home" to "Gerry" (Brad Pitt), her husband's first name. It is also here that Gerry learns of the situation, as his former boss briefs him, saying, "The airlines were the perfect delivery system." This line provides a sting for viewers, who remember that the events of September 11, 2001, were produced through airplanes. In fact, out of context, the line could easily be taken as a description of those events. The fact that Gerry is a former United Nations employee gives him a sort of transnational or even global positioning, at the same time as his Americanness serves to anchor him, his family, and the disaster within the United States. The fact that they lived in Philadelphia before the disaster, where the United States was politically constituted, is also not irrelevant to a tale about the end of the country as we knew it.

The film also reproduces an important 9/11 narrative in relation to immigrants. This narrative is first disguised as a potential coun-

ter-idea to general 9/11 articulations about immigration in the global North generally, and in the United States more particularly.
Namely, immigrants are a perceived threat to a country's security.
Jurgen Warmbrunn (Ludi Boeken), a government official in Israel,
tells Gerry, who is there trying to understand what is happening,
"The more people we let in, the fewer we have to fight." This is in
reference to a wall they built, which seemed to keep the zombies
out, but that had a checkpoint to indiscriminately let in noninfected
refugees. The wall eventually caved under the determination of the
zombies, and Israel, the last holdout, falls. The symbolism of Gerry
looking for answers in Jerusalem is, undoubtedly, a nice touch in a
tale about the apocalypse. But possibilities for the symbolism are
shattered when Jerusalem indeed falls, and it is the refugees who
"bring Jerusalem down." As refugees found themselves in the safety of Jerusalem, they began to express their relief and gratitude by
singing through bullhorns, with the noise attracting the zombies.
The final image overpowers the original idea that saving humans
was the right thing to do. The film presents viewers with other 9/11
narratives already discussed in previous chapters. For instance,
similar to *Flightplan*, viewers realize that in *World War Z*, "the
threat is on board" (and potentially everywhere), as Gerry boards a
plane from Israel to Germany, only to find, midair, that there are
zombies inside. And, as Ryan relays in *Up in the Air*, Gerry also
discovers that "movement is life."

After traveling to various parts of the world, trying to understand
what is happening and how to fight the virus, Gerry learns the most
important lesson of the film: The key to overcoming the zombie
apocalypse is to hide in plain sight—or, to camouflage one's self.
After observing their behavior in various contexts, Gerry realizes
that zombies will not touch a person with a terminal illness. This
becomes the ultimate conundrum: In order to survive, humanity
must be turned invisible by becoming ill. The film ends with Gerry's voice-over narration telling viewers, "People began to fight

back." He admonishes them with the following words, "If you can fight, fight. Be prepared for anything. Our war has just begun." This last statement provides a decisive 9/11 reference, and provides a tie-in to the initial and controversial ending of *United 93*, discussed in chapter 2: "America's war on terror had begun."

CONCLUSION

Citing Slavoj Zizek, Sherryl Vint argues, "We find it easier to imagine a total catastrophe which ends all life on earth than . . . to imagine" a somewhat smaller transformation, like a change in the capitalist system (2013, 134). And because of this, she continues, "We revel in the imagination of apocalyptic disaster in recent popular culture" (134). In his speech to the nation, shortly after the September 11, 2001, attacks, President Bush delivered what would become an emblem line for his presidency and his approach to terrorism: "We will not tire, we will not falter, and we will not fail" (Bush 2001). This line also captures the impetus behind the [white] American aggressive nationalism that Holloway (2008) references above—a particular kind of nationalism that oozes a take-charge, masculinist whiteness, and that has permeated 9/11 films, irrespective of genre and topic. Similar to other films discussed in this book, the films in this chapter share central elements revolving around whiteness. Viewers are told that the apocalypse happens to whites; it is up to white men to fight it; white men must protect their families; and the apocalypse can be managed or overcome by these men. This is why, when writing for *Variety*, Justin Chang makes the following assessment in his analysis of *Take Shelter*:

> Skillfully tapping into a nameless but all-too-familiar sense of dread, of being powerless to hold danger at bay, "Take Shelter" emerges [as] a study of troubled masculinity in a troubled world. Curtis' refusal to share his fears with his wife is infuriating, his behavior often inscrutable; yet everything he does is motivated

by an admirable determination to protect his family at any cost. Shannon's tightly wound, gruff-yet-tender performance invites sympathy even as the character's irrationality keeps the viewer off balance. (2011).

These words, while perfect to describe *Take Shelter*, can also be used to describe the men in the other two films. *Contagion*, although constituted by an ensemble cast, favors Mitch's character, who is trying to protect his daughter (the only other surviving member of his family) from the disease. *World War Z* shows Gerry trying to protect his wife and two daughters. The fact that these characters are white men protecting white women is part of both Hollywood's historical representations and its 9/11 understanding of security and protection. More importantly, the fact that whatever these men do must be seen as admirable, even when their acts are infuriating (recall that even Oskar does not tell his mother about his father's answering machine messages), reflects 9/11 discourse around not faltering in the quest to fight threats to Americanness.

Take Shelter director Nichols expresses this sentiment best, when he candidly explains how his own anxieties informed the film. In an interview with Nigel Smith, he states:

> I was moving from my 20s into my 30s. I had just gotten married and my first film had done all right. I finally had something to lose. The anxiety grew out of that. Not to mention, shit was going crazy: Bush was in the White House, the economy was collapsing, there were wars everywhere, towns were getting destroyed by storms. It was just like, what's going on? It felt like the world at large was losing its grasp of keeping everything together. That was just in the air. It still is. (Smith 2011)

As mentioned above, for anyone familiar with Bible stories, *Take Shelter* has a strong allusion to the story of Noah's Ark, connecting viewers' anxieties to cemented religious tales. *World War Z* and *Contagion* present viewers with an appeal to history, for both explicitly cite the case of the Spanish flu in 1918 as a precedent for the spread of a disease at unparalleled levels. The allusion to the Spanish flu serves to ground the plot of the films in history, but also it serves as a cautionary tale: If something like that could happen in 1918, prior to the technology we have today, and even prior to the first transatlantic flight, just imagine what such an event would do to humanity today. These efforts seek to position the films within viewers' cultural knowledge, but they also convey that regardless of how unprecedented viewers might consider an event to be, it *can* be connected to mythology or history.

On a basic level, the connection to cultural elements and history provides continuity between the fictional scenarios in these films and viewers' understandings of reality. More importantly, this connection suggests that events such as those taking place on September 11, 2001, can be tied to mythology and history, placing them within the continuum of human history. This is why we are somewhat skeptical of Walliss and Aston's assertion that "if post-9/11 apocalyptic movies routinely [critique] the existing status quo and socio-political order, then they also [present] a narrative that completely rejects and severs ties with the past in order to begin again" (2011, 60). We suggest that in the end, 9/11 apocalyptic films do not break all ties with the past, for although they embody, portray, and promote current ideologies about threat, uncertainty, insecurity, race, gender, and citizenship, oftentimes these ideologies are grounded in pre-9/11 conceptions of history and (social) development. They also document our fears and even our actions, many of which are the result of historical continuities.

These continuities have been central to our project here, which as we discussed in chapter 1, is guided by Feagin's *white racial frame* and Wingfield's *systemic gendered racism*. Both inform our conception of the *9/11 project* and highlight continuing and persistent impacts of "racial stereotypes, prejudices, ideologies, images, interpretations and narratives, emotions . . . reactions to language accents, [and] racialized inclinations to discriminate" (Feagin 2010,

3), as well as ways in which "racist ideology, racist imagery, and racist institutions . . . allow systemic racism to flourish [as] gendered" (Wingfield 2009, 7). Also evident in 9/11 apocalyptic films are a collection of long-festering fears infused by, as Feagin conveys, images, emotions, and narratives about the virtues and dominance ("an overarching worldview") of white, male Americanness along with the precarious otherness of those not included in this category. That this worldview is raced, as well as gendered, reminds us that the *white racial frame* and *systemic gendered racism* are historical in scope, while as components of the *9/11 project*, they also have specific inflections in a world after September 11, 2001.

In closing, we would like to call attention to and reiterate the perilous position of those othered within the *9/11 project*. This position becomes dreadfully apparent and all the more daunting when considering the sentiment expressed by former President Bush in the chapter's opening epigraph, in which the president ominously muses that in the end "we may be the only ones left." His words illustrate the new inflections we have analyzed throughout this book and lend expression to what might be termed "9/11 global systemic gendered racism." Moreover, his words resonate with a population fearful of the world's ultimate demise, since on an otherwise beautiful Tuesday morning over a decade ago, many Americans thought they were experiencing the beginnings of that demise. During the past decade, Hollywood mainstream films have suggested to mainstream viewers, often reassuringly, that they (and others who look like them) might very well be the only ones left. In the conclusion to his book *The Rhetoric of Terror*, Redfield calls for hope of "a future that [will] no longer be apocalyptic: a peace that [will] no longer be a war on terror" (2009, 95). As we end *Projecting 9/11*, we can only join him in this hope, even if within the current landscape, Hollywood seems to have other aims and projects in production.

Bibliography

Amago, Samuel. 2010. Ethics, Aesthetics, and the Future in Alfonso Carron's *Children of Men*. *Discourse* 32 (2): 212–35.

Ander, Steve, and Art Swift. 2013. "See Something, Say Something" Unfamiliar to Most Americans. *Gallup Politics.com*, Dec. 23. Retrieved Feb. 27, 2014, from http://www.gallup.com/poll/166622/something-say-something-unfamiliar-americans.aspx.

Anderson, Lisa. 1997. *Mammies No More: The Changing Image of Black Women on Stage and Screen*. New York: Rowman & Littlefield.

Anonymous. 2013. Apocalyptic Movies.com. Retrieved Aug. 18, 2013, from http://www.apocalypticmovies.com/movie-index/2000s.html.

Aslan, Reza. 2010. Foreword. In *Reframing 9/11: Film, Popular Culture and the "War on Terror,"* ed. Jeff Birkenstein, Anna Froula, and Karen Randell, xi–xiii. New York: Continuum.

Associated Press. 2006. Once a Mystery, 9/11 Rescuer Unmasks Self amid Publicity for New Film. *USA Today*, Aug. 15. Retrieved Sept. 23, 2013, from http://www.usatoday.com/news/nation/2006-08-15-sept11-hero_x.htm.

Baum, Bruce. 2011. Hollywood's Crisis of Capitalism 2011: Inside Job, The Company Men, and the Myth of a Good Capitalism. *New Political Science* 33 (4): 603–12.

Beck, Bernard. 2011. No Company for Old Men: Adventures in Unemployment in *The Company Men*. *Multicultural Perspectives* 13 (4): 205–8.

Bell-Metereau, Rebecca. 2004. The How-To Manual, the Prequel and the Sequel in Post 9/11Cinema. In *Film and Television after 9/11*, ed. Wheeler W. Dixon, 142–62. Carbondale: Southern Illinois University Press.

Beltran, Mary. 2009. *Latina/o Stars in U.S. Eyes: The Making and Meanings of Film and TV Stardom*. Champaign: University of Illinois Press.

Berg, Charles Ramírez. 2002. *Latino Images in Film: Stereotypes, Subversion, and Resistance*. Austin: University of Texas Press.

Bernardi, Daniel. 2001. *Classic Hollywood, Classic Whiteness*. Minneapolis: University of Minnesota Press.

Bierly, Mandi, Jason Clark, Clark Collis, Steve Daly, Neil Drumming, Jeff Jensen, Paul Katz, Jeff LaBrecque, Chris Nashawaty, Tim Purtell, Joshua Rich, Erin Richter, Josh Rettenberg, Christine Spines, Bejami Svetkey, and Alice Lee Tebo. 2006. The 25 Most Controversial Movies Ever. *Entertainment Weekly*, June 16. Retrieved Sept. 23, 2013, from http://www.ew.com/ew/article/0,1202224,00.html.

Birch-Bayley, Nicole. 2012. Terror in Horror Genres: The Global Media and the Millennial Zombie. *Journal of Popular Culture* 45 (6): 1137–51.

Birkenstein, Jeff, Anna Froula, and Karen Randell, eds. 2010. *Reframing 9/11: Film, Popular Culture and the "War on Terror."* New York: Continuum.

Bishop, Kyle. 2009. Dead Man Still Walking: Explaining the Zombie Renaissance. *Journal of Popular Film and Television* 37 (1): 16–25.

Bloodsworth-Lugo, Mary K. and Carmen R. Lugo-Lugo. 2010. *Containing (Un)American Bodies: Race, Sexuality, and Post-9/11 Constructions of Citizenship*. New York: Rodopi Press.

Bogle, Donald. 2001. *Toms, Coons, Mulattoes, Mammies, and Bucks: An Interpretative History of Blacks in American Films*. 4th. ed. New York: Continuum.

Bond, Marybeth. 2012. Women Travel Statistics Explained by Travel Expert. *The Gutsy Traveler.com*, Apr. 17. Retrieved Feb. 27, 2014, from http://gutsytraveler.com/women-travel-statistics-2/.

Brown, Alyssa. 2013. In U.S., Standard of Living Perceptions Hit Five-Year High. *Gallup.com*, May 10. Retrieved Feb. 27, 2014, from http://www.gallup.com/poll/162392/standard-living-perceptions-hit-five-year-high.aspx.

Bush, George W. 2001. Address to the Nation. *Presidential Rhetoric.com*, Sept. 20. Retrieved Sept. 23, 2013, from http://www.presidentialrhetoric.com/speeches/09.20.01.html.

——. 2002a. State of the Union. *Presidential Rhetoric.com*, Jan. 29. Retrieved Sept. 23, 2013, from http://www.presidentialrhetoric.com/speeches/01.29.02.html.

——. 2002b. The Iraqi Threat. *American Rhetoric: The Rhetoric of 9/11*, Oct. 7. Retrieved Sept. 23, 2013, from http://www.presidentialrhetoric.com/speeches/10.7.02. html.

——. 2002c. Homeland Security Act. *American Rhetoric: The Rhetoric of 9/11*, Nov. 25. Retrieved Sept. 23, 2013, from http://www.presidentialrhetoric.com/speeches/11.25.02. html.

——. 2003. Text of President Bush's 2003 State of the Union Address. *Washington Post.com*, Jan. 28. Retrieved Feb. 27, 2014, from http://www.washingtonpost.com/wp-srv/onpolitics/transcripts/bushtext_012803.html.

——. 2004. Text of President Bush's 2004 State of the Union Address. *Washington Post.com*, Jan. 20. Retrieved Feb. 27, 2014, from http://www.washingtonpost.com/wp-srv/politics/transcripts/bushtext_012004.html.

Carroll, Joseph. 2005. Bird Flu Concerns Rise as Most Urgent Health Problem. *Gallup.com*, Nov. 18. Retrieved Feb. 27, 2014, from http://www.gallup.com/poll/20032/Bird-Flu-Concerns-Rise-Most-Urgent-Health-Problem.aspx.

——. 2007. Just 4 in 10 Americans Say Recession Is Likely Next Year. *Gallup.com*, Nov.7. Retrieved Feb. 27, 2014, from http://www.gallup.com/poll/102487/Just-Americans-Say-Recession-Likely-Next-Year.aspx#2.

Chang, Justin. 2011. Review: Take Shelter. *Variety*, Jan. 25. Retrieved Sept. 23, 2013, from http://variety.com/2011/film/reviews/take-shelter-1117944389/.

Charity, Tom. 2009. Review: *Avatar* Delivers on the Hype. *CNN.com*, Dec. 18. Retrieved Sept. 23, 2013, from http://www.cnn.com/2009/SHOWBIZ/Movies/12/17/avatar. review/index.html.

Chernus, Ira. 2006. *Monsters to Destroy: The Neoconservative War on Terror and Sin*. Boulder, CO: Paradigm Publishers.

Clover, Joshua. 2011. Fall and Rise. *Film Quarterly* 65 (2). Retrieved Sept. 23, 2013, from http://www.filmquarterly.org/2012/01/fall-and-rise/.

CNN.com. 2005. Human Bird Flu in China, One Dead. *CNN.com*, Nov. 17. Retrieved Feb. 27, 2014, from http://www.cnn.com/2005/HEALTH/conditions/11/16/bird.flu.china/.

——. 2013. CNN Poll: 62% Say Border Security Needs to Be First Priority in Immigration Policy. *CNN.com*, June 18. Retrieved Feb. 27, 2014, from https://www.numbersusa/ com/content/news/june-18-2013/ cnn-poll-62-say-border-security-needs-be-first-priority-immigration-policy.html.

——. 2014. Avian Flu Fast Facts. *CNN.com*. Feb. 2. Retrieved Feb. 27, 2014, from http://www.cnn.com/2013/08/23/health/avian-flu-fast-facts/.

Corliss, Richard. 2006. Let's Roll!: Inside the Making of *United 93. Time*, Apr. 9. Retrieved Sept. 23, 2013, from http://www.time.com/time/magazine/article/0,9171,1181589,00.html.

Curth, Traci. 2006. Film Trailer Brings Back Sept. 11 Shock. *Toledo Free Press*, Apr. 26. Retrieved Sept. 23, 2013, from http://www.toledofreepress.com/2006/04/26/film-trailer-brings-back-sept-11-shock/.

Dargis, Manohla. 2005. Hunting for a Child No One Believes Is There. *New York Times,* Sept. 23. Retrieved Jan. 6, 2012, http://movies.nytimes.com/2005/09/23/movies/ 23flig.html.

Denby, David. 2011. Call the Doctor: *Contagion. The New Yorker*, Sept. 19. Retrieved Sept. 23, 2013, from http://www.newyorker.com/arts/critics/cinema/2011/09/19/110919crci_ cinema_denby?currentPage=2.

——. 2013. Life and Undead. *The New Yorker*. July 1. Retrieved Sept. 23, 2013, from http://www.newyorker.com/arts/critics/cinema/2013/07/01/130701crci_ cinema_denby.

Department of Homeland Security. 2010. About DHS. *Department of Homeland Security*. Retrieved Apr. 19, 2014, from http://www.dhs.gov/about-dhs.

Dixon, Wheeler W. 2004. Something Lost: Film after 9/11. In *Film and Television after 9/11*, ed. Wheeler W. Dixon, 1–28. Carbondale: Southern Illinois University Press.

Dugan, Andrew. 2013. On 10th Anniversary, 53% in U.S. See Iraq War as Mistake. *Gallup.com*, Mar. 18. Retrieved Feb. 27, 2014, from http://www. gallup.com/poll/161399/10th-Anniversary-iraq-war-mistake.aspx.

Ebert, Roger. 2010. *Wall Street: Money Never Sleeps. RogerEbert.com*, Sept. 22. Retrieved Sept. 23, 2013, from http://www.rogerebert.com/reviews/wall-street-money-never-sleeps-2010.

Feagin, Joe R. 2010. *The White Racial Frame: Centuries of Racial Framing and Counter-Framing.* New York: Routledge.

Fine, Marshall. 2011. Huff Post Review: *Larry Crowne. Huffington Post*, June 29. Retrieved Sept. 23, 2013, from http://www.huffingtonpost.com/marshall-fine/huffpost-review-ilarry-cr_b_886738.html.

Flores, Lucien. 2013. Interview: World War Z Director Marc Forster. *Daily Free Press*, June 21. Retrieved Sept. 23, 2013, from http://dailyfreepress.com/2013/06/21/interview-marc-forster-chases-zombies-in-world-war-z/.

Fuller, Karla Rae, and Tom Gunning. 2010. *Hollywood Goes Oriental: Cauc-Asian Performance in American Film.* Detroit: Wayne State University Press.

Gallup. 2013. Parties in Congress. *Gallup.com*. Retrieved Jan. 12, 2014, from http://www.gallup.com/poll/24649/Parties-Congress.aspx.

———. 2014. Terrorism in the United States. *Gallup.com*, Mar. 22. Retrieved Feb. 27, 2014, from http://www.gallup.com/poll/4909/Terrorism-United-States-aspx#1.

Gilbey, Ryan. 2010. The Money Will Roll Right In. *New Statesman*, Sept. 30. Retrieved May 26, 2013, from http://www.newstatesman.com/film/2010/10/wall-street-money-gekko-film.

Giroux, Henry. 1999. *The Mouse That Roared: Disney and the End of Innocence.* Lanham, MD: Rowman & Littlefield.

Gleiberman, Owen. 2010. Movie Review: *The Company Men. Entertainment Weekly*, Dec. 3. Retrieved May 31, 2013, from http://www.ew.com/ew/article/0,20446275,00.html.

Goldwag, Arthur. 2009. The Nature and Purpose of Conspiracy Theories. *Arthur Goldwag*, Dec. 11. Retrieved Sept. 23, 2013, from http://arthurgoldwag. wordpress.com/2009/12/11/the-nature-and-purpose-of-conspiracy-theories/.

Grewal, Inderpal. 2003. Transnational America: Race, Gender, and Citizenship after 9/11. *Social Identities: Journal for the Study of Race, Nation, and Culture*, 9 (4): 535–61.

Heller, Dana. 2005. *The Selling of 9/11: How a National Tragedy Became a Commodity.* New York: Palgrave MacMillan.

Higgins, Gareth. 2012. Hope Three Ways. *Sojourners*, 41 (2): 39.

Hoffman, Jordan. 2011. Steven Soderbergh Interview. *Ugo.com*, Sept. 7. Retrieved Sept. 23, 2013, from http://www.ugo.com/movies/steven-soderbergh-interview.

Holden, Stephen. 2010. Perils of the Corporate Ladder: It Hurts When You Fall. *New York Times,* Dec. 9. Retrieved May 31, 2013, from http://movies.nytimes. com/ 2010/12/10/movies/10company.html?pagewanted=all&_r=0.

——. 2011. Larry Crowne: Stymied in Middle Age, Reaching for a New Life. *New York Times*, June 30. Retrieved Sept. 23, 2013, from http://movies. nytimes.com/2001/07/01/movies/tom-hanks-and-julia-roberts-in-larry-crowne-review.html.

Holloway, David. 2008. *Cultures of the War on Terror: Empire, Ideology and the Remaking of 9/11*. Montreal: McGill-Queens University Press.

IMDb. 2012. *United 93*. *IMDB.com*. Retrieved Sept. 23, 2013, from http://www. imdb.com/ title/tt0475276/.

Infoshop.org. 2010. Strangers in a Tangled Wilderness. Authors on Anarchism—An Interview with Alan Moore. Infoshop News. Retrieved Sept. 24, 2013, from http://news.infoshop.org/ article.php?story=2007alan-moore-interview.

Jackson, Richard. 2009. The 9/11 Attacks and the Social Construction of a National Narrative. In *The Impact of 9/11 on the Media, Arts, and Entertainment: The Day That Changed Everything?*, ed. Matthew J. Morgan, 25–35. New York: Palgrave Macmillan.

Jernigan, Joy. 2012. World's Worst Tourists? Americans say . . . Americans. *NBC News.com*, Mar. 2. Retrieved Feb. 27, 2014, from http://www.nbcnews. com/travel/ worlds-worst-tourists-americans-say-americans-293837.

Jones, Jeffrey. 2007. Eight in 10 Say Leaders Pay Too Little Attention to Veterans. *Gallup.com*, Apr. 25. Retrieved Feb. 27, 2014, from http://www.gallup. com/poll/27310/Eight-Say-Leaders-Pay-Too-Little-Attention-Veterans.aspx.

——. 2010. Americans Give GOP Edge on Most Election Issues. *Gallup.com*. Retrieved Jan. 12, 2014, from http://www.gallup.com/poll/142730/ Americans-Give-GOP-Edge-Election-Issues.aspx.

——. 2011. One in Four Americans Say Lives Permanently Changed by 9/11. *Gallup.com*, Sept. 8. Retrieved Feb. 27, 2014, from http://www.gallup.com/ poll/149366/ One-Four-Americans-Say-Lives-Permanently-Changed.aspx.

Kellner, Douglas. 2011. *Cinema Wars: Hollywood Films and Politics in the Bush-Cheney Era*. Hoboken, NJ: Wiley-Blackwell.

King, Claire S. 2010. The Man Inside: Trauma, Gender and the Nation in *The Brave One*. *Critical Studies in Media Communication* 27 (2): 11–30.

King, C. Richard, Carmen R. Lugo-Lugo, and Mary K. Bloodsworth-Lugo. 2010. *Animating Difference: Race, Gender, and Sexuality in Contemporary Films for Children*. Lanham, MD: Rowman & Littlefield.

Levina, Marina, and Diem-My T. Bui. 2013. Introduction: Toward a Comprehensive Monster Theory in the 21st Century. In *Monster Culture in the 21st Century: A Reader*, ed. Marina Levina and Diem-My T. Bui. London: Bloomsbury.

Lincoln, Jamie. 2013. Marc Forster: The Eye of the Swarm. *Interview*, June 20. Retrieved Sept. 23, 2013, from http://www.interviewmagazine.com/film/ marc-forster-world-war-z#_.

Lowrey, Annie. 2013. Weath Gap Among Races Has Widened Since Recession. *New York Times*, April 28. Retrieved Aug. 16, 2014, from http://www. nytimes.com/2013/04/29/business/racial-wealth-gap-widened-during-recession.html?pagewanted=all.

Margolin, Josh. 2013. Exclusive: After Westgate, Interpol Chief Ponders "Armed Citizenry." *ABC News.com*, Oct. 21. Retrieved Feb. 27, 2014, from http://abcnews.go.com/Blotter/Exclusive-westgate-interpol-chief-ponders-armed-citizenry/story?id=20637341&singlePage=true.

Marin, Rick. 2011. Can Manhood Survive the Recession? *Newsweek*, Apr. 17. Retrieved Apr. 19, 2014, from http://www.newsweek.com/can-manhood-survive-recession-66607.

Markert, John. 2011. *Post-9/11 Cinema: Through a Lens Darkly*. Lanham, MD: Scarecrow Press.

Markovitz, Jonathan. 2004. Reel Terror Post 9/11. In *Film and Television after 9/11*, ed. Wheeler W. Dixon, 201–25. Carbondale: Southern Illinois University Press.

Martelle, Scott. 2006. Theater Pulls "United 93" Trailer after Complaints. *Los Angeles Times*, Apr. 5. Retrieved Sept. 23, 2013, from http://articles.latimes.com/2006/apr/05/entertainment/et-united5.

McCarthy, Thomas. 2010. *Race, Empire, and the Idea of Human Development*. Cambridge, UK: Cambridge University Press.

Melnick, Jeffrey. 2009. *9/11 Culture*. Hoboken, NJ: Wiley-Blackwell.

Memmi Albert. 2000. *Racism*. Translated by Steve Martinot. Minneapolis: University of Minnesota Press.

Mitchell, Edward. 2012. *Up in the Air. Journal of Architectural Education*, 66 (1): 9–12.

Mohney, Gillian. 2010. John Wells' *The Company Men*: Beyond the Gray Flannel Suit. *Interview*. Retrieved May 29, 2013, from http://www.interviewmagazine.com/film/john-wells-company-men.

Morales, Lymari. 2012. Americans' Immigration Concerns Linger. *Gallup.com*, Jan.17. Retrieved Feb. 27, 2014, from http://www.gallup.com/poll/152072/Americans-immigration-concerns-linger.aspx.

Nagourney, Adam. 2008. Obama Elected President as Racial Barrier Falls. *New York Times*, Nov. 8. Retrieved Jan. 12, 2014, from http://www.nytimes.com/2008/11/05/us/politics/05Select.html?pagewanted=all.

Neuman, Clayton, and Rebecca Winters Keegan. 2006. Let's Roll!: Inside the Making of *United 93. Time*, Apr. 9. Retrieved Sept. 24, 2013, from http://content.time.com/time/ magazine/article/0,9171,1181589,00.html.

Nocera, Joe. 2010. When Did Gekko Get So Toothless? *New York Times*, Sept. 23. Retrieved June 7, 2013, from http://www.nytimes.com/2010/09/26/movies/26wall.html?pagewanted=all&_r=0.

Novikov, Eugene. 2006. World Trade Center. *Film Blather*. Retrieved Sept. 24, 2013, from http://filmblather.com/Filmsworldtradecenter/.

Oprah Magazine. 2010. Up in the Air's Jason Reitman. *Oprah.com*, Jan. 29. Retrieved May 27, 2013, from http://www.oprah.com/entertainment/Up-in-the-Air-Director-Jason-Reitman/1.

Pellicer, Juan. 2010. Bridging Worlds: Transtextuality, Montage, and the Poetics of *Babel. Mexican Studies/Estudion Mexicanos* 26 (2): 239–49.

People Press.org. 2013. Most Say Illegal Immigrants Should Be Allowed to Stay, But Citizenship Is More Divisive. *Pew Research Center.org*, Mar. 28. Retrieved Feb. 27, 2014, from http://www.people-press.org/2013/03/28/most-say-illegal-immigrants-should-be-allowed-sto-stay-but-citizenship-is-more-divisive/#overview.

Phillips, Michael. 2011. Strong Effort Yields Merely Adequate "Company" : Great Cast in the Service of a So-So Movie. *Chicago Tribune*, Jan. 20. Retrieved Apr. 19, 2014, from http://articles.chicagotribune.com/2011-01-20/entertainment/sc-mov-1209-company-men-20110120-1_1_bobby-mad-men-cast.

Pollard, Thomas. 2009. Hollywood 9/11: Time of Crisis. In *The Impact of 9/11 on the Media, Arts, and Entertainment: The Day That Changed Everything?*, ed. Matthew J. Morgan, 195–207. New York: Palgrave Macmillan.

PopSugar Entertainment. 2009. Buzz Interview: Jason Reitman Talks Clooney and *Up in the Air*. *PopSugar Entertainment*, Nov. 30. Retrieved May 27, 2013, from http://www.Buzzsugar/com/Exclusive-Interview-Director-Jason-Reitman-About-Up-Air-6465092.

Presidential Rhetoric.com. 2013. Speeches from George W. Bush's Second Term. Retrieved Dec. 18, 2013, from http://www.presidentialrhetoric.com/speeches/bush_secondterm. html.

Randell, Karen. 2010. " It Was Like a Movie" : The Impossibility of Representation in Oliver Stone's World Trade Center. In *Reframing 9/11: Film, Popular Culture and the "War on Terror*," ed. Jeff Berkenstein, Anna Froula, and Karen Randell, 141–52. New York: Continuum.

Redfield, Marc. 2009. *The Rhetoric of Terror: Reflections on 9/11 and the War on Terror*. New York: Fordham University Press.

Rich, Ruby. 2004. After the Fall: Cinema Studies after Post 9/11. *Cinema Journal* 43 (2): 109–15.

Robertson, Barbara. 2011. *Rango*: Industrial Light and Magic Animators Turn Gore Verbinski's Vision into Acclaimed Animated Feature. *Animation Mentor.com*, March. Retrieved Sept. 24, 2013, from http://newsletters. animationmentor.com/newsletter/0311/feature.html.

Rodríquez, Clara. 2004. *Heroes, Lovers, and Others: The Story of Latinos in Hollywood*. Washington, DC: Smithsonian Books.

Roediger, David R. 2005. *Working toward Whiteness: How America's Immigrants Became White*. New York: Basic Books.

Saad, Lydia. 2005. Americans Predict Avian Flu Will Reach the U.S. *Gallup.com*, Nov. 4. Retrieved Feb. 27, 2014, from http://www.gallup.com/poll/19585/Americans-Predict-Avian-Flu-Will-Reach-US.aspx.

———. 2010. U.S. Workers Still Haven't Shaken the Job Worries of 2009. *Gallup.com*, Sept. 2. Retrieved Feb. 27, 2014, from http://www.gallup.com/poll/164222/workers-havent-shaken-job-worries-2009.aspx.

———. 2013. Federal Debt, Terrorism Considered Top Threats to U.S. *Gallup.com*. Retrieved Jan. 12, 2014, from http://www/gallup.com/poll/139385/Federal-Debt-Terrorism-Considered-Top-Threats.aspx.

Sanchez-Escalonilla, Antonio. 2010. Hollywood and the Rhetoric of Panic: The Popular Genres of Action and Fantasy in the Wake of the 9/11 Attacks. *Journal of Popular Film and Television* 38 (1): 10–20.

Schopp, Andrew. 2009. Interrogating the Manipulation of Fear: *V for Vendetta*, *Batman Begins*, *Good Night, and Good Luck*, and America's War on Terror. In *The War on Terror and American Popular Culture: September 11 and Beyond*, ed. Andrew Schopp and Mathew B. Hill, 259–86. Madison, NJ: Fairleigh Dickinson University Press.

Schopp, Andrew, and Matthew B. Hill. 2009. Introduction: The Curious Knot. In *The War on Terror and American Popular Culture: September 11 and Beyond*, ed. Andrew Schopp and Mathew B. Hill, 11–42. Madison, NJ: Fairleigh Dickinson University Press.

Schorr, Daniel. 2008. A New, "Post-Racial" Political Era in America. *NPR.com*, Jan. 28. Retrieved Jan. 12, 2014, from http://www.npr.org/templates/story/story.php?storyId= 18489466.

Scott, A. O. 2008. Lurking in the Shadows of Suburbia, a Menacing Neighbor with a Gun. *New York Times*, Sept. 19. Retrieved Jan. 5, 2012, from http://movies.nytimes.com/2008/09/ 19/movies/19terr.html.

——. 2011. Take Shelter. *New York Times*, Sept. 29. Retrieved Sept. 24, 2013, from http://movies.nytimes.com/2011/09/30/movies/take-shelter-with-michael-shannon-and-jessica-chastain.html.

Sklar, Robert. 1994. *Movie-Made America: A Cultural History of American Movies*. New York: Vintage Books.

Smith, Nigel. 2011. Interview: *Take Shelter* Director Jeff Nichols on How to Make an Indie Epic. *IndieWire.com*, Sept. 28. Retrieved Sept. 24, 2013, from http://www.indiewire.com/ article/interview_take_shelter_director_jeff_nichols_on_making_an_indie_epic_and_th.

Snauwaert, Dale T. 2004. The Bush Doctrine and Just War Theory. *The Online Journal of Peace and Conflict Resolution* 6 (1): 121–35. Retrieved Sept. 24, 2013, from http://www.trinstitute.org/ojpcr/6_1snau.pdf.

Taylor, Paul, Cary Funk, and Peyton Craighill. 2006. Looking Backward and Forward, Americans See Less Progress in Their Lives. *Pew Research Center.org*, Oct. 10. Retrieved Feb. 27, 2014, from http://pewsocialtrends.org/files/2010/10/Ladder.pdf.

Todd, Deborah M. 2006. *World Trade Center* Omits Black Soldier. *Pittsburgh Courier*. Retrieved Sept. 24, 2013, from http://newpittsburghcourieronline.com/articlelive/articles/35730/1/World-Trade-Center-omits-Black-soldier/WTC-movies-unsung-hero.html.

Travers, Peter. 2011. *Larry Crowne. Rolling Stone*, June 7. Retrieved Sept. 24, 2013, from http://www.rollingstone.com/movies/reviews/larry-crowne-20110707.

Turner, Graeme. 2006. *Film as Social Practice IV*. New York: Routledge.

Van Ginneken, Jaap. 2007. *Screening Difference: How Hollywood's Blockbuster Films Imagine Race, Ethnicity, and Culture*. Lanham, MD: Rowman & Littlefield.

Vera, Hernán, and Andrew Gordon. 2003. *Screen Saviors: Hollywood Fictions of Whiteness*. Lanham, MD: Rowman & Littlefield.

Vint, Sherryl. 2013. Abject Posthumanism: Neoliberalism, Biopolitics, and Zombies. In *Monster Culture in the 21st Century: A Reader*, ed. Marina Leina and Diem-My T. Buy, 133–46. London: Bloomsbury.

Walliss, John, and James Aston. 2011. Doomsday America: The Pessimistic Turn of Post-9/11 Apocalyptic Cinema. *Journal of Religion and Popular Culture* 23 (1): 53–64.

Walsh, Richard. 2010. The Horror, The Horror: What Kind of (Horror) Movie Is the Apocalypse? *Journal of Religion and Popular Culture* 22 (3).

Weintraub, Steve. 2011. Tom Hanks and Julia Roberts Interview: Larry Crowne. *The Collider*, July 5. Retrieved Sept. 24, 2013, from http://collider.com/tom-hanks-julia-roberts-interview-larry-crowne/.

Wingfield, Adia Harvey. 2009. *Doing Business with Beauty: Black Women, Hair Salons, and the Racial Enclave Economy*. Lanham, MD: Rowman & Littlefield.

Woodward, Bob, and Dan Balz. 2002. At Camp David, Advise and Dissent; Bush, Aides Grapple with War Plans. *Washington Post*, Jan. 31.

Worstall, Tim. 2012. The Great Recession Is Just Like the Great Depression. *Forbes*, Nov. 7. Retrieved Sept. 24, 2013, from http://www/forbes/com/sites/timworstall/2012/11/07/ the-great-recession-is-just-like-the-great-depression/.

WP Politics. 2013. *Washington Post* Poll. *Washington Post.com*, Apr. 18. Retrieved Feb. 27, 2014. http://www.washingtonpost.com/wp-srv/politics/polls/postpoll_20130418.html.

Filmography

Avatar. Dir. James Cameron. Twentieth Century Fox Film Corporation, December 18, 2009.

Babel. Dir. Alejandro González Iñárritu. Paramount Pictures, November 10, 2006.

Brave One, The. Dir. Neil Jordan. Warner Bros. Pictures, September 14, 2007.

Brothers. Dir. Jim Sheridan. Lionsgate, December 4, 2009.

Children of Men. Dir. Alfonso Cuarón. Universal Pictures, January 5, 2007.

Company Men, The. Dir. John Wells. The Weinstein Company, March 11, 2011.

Contagion. Dir. Steven Soderbergh. Warner Bros. Pictures, September 9, 2011.

Day After, The. Dir. Nicholas Meyer, American Broadcasting Company (ABC), November 20, 1983.

Dawn of the Dead. Dir. George A. Ramero. United Film Distribution Company, May 24, 1979.

Dracula. Dir. Tod Browning and Karl Freund. Universal Pictures, February 14, 1931.

Eat Pray Love. Dir. Ryan Murphy. Columbia Pictures, August 13, 2010.

Extremely Loud & Incredibly Close. Dir. Stephen Daldry. Paramount Pictures, January 20, 2012.

Flight Plan. Dir. Robert Schwentke. Buena Vista Pictures, September 23, 2005.

Home of the Brave. Dir. Irwin Winkler. Metro-Goldwyn-Mayer (MGM), March 1, 2007.

Hurt Locker, The. Dir. Kathryn Bigelow. Summit Entertainment, June 26, 2009.

Lakeview Terrace. Dir. Neil LaBute. Screen Gems, September 19, 2008.

Larry Crowne. Dir. Tom Hanks. Universal Pictures, July 1, 2011.

Lions for Lambs. Dir. Robert Redford. Metro-Goldwyn-Mayer (MGM), November 9, 2007.

Lucky Ones, The. Dir. Neil Burger. Lionsgate, September 26, 2008.

Planet 51. Dir. Jorge Blanco, Javier Abad, and Marcos Martinez. Ilion Animation, November 20, 2009.

Princess and the Frog, The. Dir. Ron Clements and John Musker. Walt Disney Animation Studios, December 11, 2009.

Rio. Dir. Carlos Saldanha. Twentieth Century Fox Animation, April 8, 2011.

Stop-Loss. Dir. Kimberly Peirce. Paramount Pictures, March 28, 2008.

Take Shelter. Dir. Jeff Nichols. Sony Pictures Classics, September 30, 2011.

Toy Story, Dir. John Lasseter. Pixar Animation Studios, November 22, 1995.

True Lies. Dir. James Cameron. Twentieth Century Fox Film Corporation, July 15, 1994.

28 Days Later. Dir. Danny Boyle. Twentieth Century Fox Film Corporation, June 27, 2003.

United 93. Dir. Paul Greengrass. Universal Pictures, April 28, 2006.

Up in the Air. Dir. Jason Reitman. Paramount Pictures, December 23, 2009.

V for Vendetta. Dir. James McTeigue. Warner Bros. Pictures, March 17, 2006.

Wall Street. Dir. Oliver Stone. Twentieth Century Fox Film Corporation, December 11, 1987.

Wall Street: Money Never Sleeps. Dir. Oliver Stone. Dune Entertainment, September 24, 2010.

War of the Worlds. Dir. Byron Haskin. Paramount Pictures, August 26, 1953.

World Trade Center. Dir. Oliver Stone. Paramount Pictures, August 9, 2006.

World War Z. Dir. Marc Forster. Paramount Pictures, June 21, 2013.

Zero Dark Thirty. Dir. Kathryn Bigelow. Columbia Pictures, January 11, 2013.

Index

About the Authors

Mary K. Bloodsworth-Lugo is professor of critical culture, gender, and race studies at Washington State University. **Carmen R. Lugo-Lugo** is associate professor of critical culture, gender, and race studies at Washington State University. Together they are the authors of *Animating Difference*, with C. Richard King.